Judgment and Promise

Judgment and Promise

An interpretation of the book of Jeremiah

J. G. McConville

Lecturer in Old Testament
Wycliffe Hall, Oxford

APOLLOS

Leicester, England

EISENBRAUNS

Winona Lake, Indiana, USA

APOLLOS (an imprint of Inter-Varsity Press),
38 De Montfort Street, Leicester LE1 7GP, England

Eisenbrauns, Inc.
Winona Lake, Indiana 46590, USA

First published 1993

British Library Cataloguing in Publication Data
A catalogue record for this book is available from the British Library.

Apollos ISBN 0–85111–431–8

Eisenbrauns ISBN 0–931464–81–1

Set in Linotron Baskerville

Typeset in Great Britain by Parker Typesetting Service, Leicester

Printed in England by Clays Ltd, St Ives plc

Contents

For Walter and Betty McConville

Preface

The present volume was begun during an extended sabbatical from Trinity College, Bristol, in 1984. I am grateful to my then colleagues for making the arrangements necessary to allow for my long absence.

The extension to the sabbatical was made possible by a grant from Tyndale House, Cambridge, who supported me further in 1989–91, in an arrangement with Wycliffe Hall, Oxford (my present employer), which allowed me time to complete the project. I am grateful also, therefore, both to the Council of Tyndale House, and to my present colleagues at Wycliffe Hall, for this further conspiracy.

My original studies were undertaken, partly, at the Ecole Biblique in Jerusalem, and the Ecumenical Institute for Theological Research, Tantur, Jerusalem. I owe thanks to the British Trust for Tantur, for financial assistance which made my stay there possible.

My interest in Jeremiah arose in the first place from my studies in Deuteronomy, which seemed to lead naturally to the prophet from Anathoth, and also from a course taught at Trinity College, Bristol. My studies in Jeremiah have been both challenging and satisfying. I offer this volume in the hope that it might help others both to enjoy the book and to be confronted by the passion of the prophet.

Oxford, May 1992   *J. G. McConville*

List of abbreviations

AB	Anchor Bible.
ATD	Das alte Testament Deutsch.
ANE	Ancient Near East(ern).
AThANT	Abhandlungen zur Theologie des Alten und Neuen Testaments.
BA	*Biblical Archaeologist.*
BWANT	Beiträge zur Wissenschaft vom Alten und Neuen Testament.
BZAW	*Beihefte zur Zeitschrift für die alttestamentliche Wissenschaft.*
CBQ	*Catholic Biblical Quarterly.*
DtH	The Deuteronomistic History.
D.	Deuteronomist.
EVV	English versions.
FRLANT	Forschung zur Religion und Literatur des Alten und Neuen Testaments.
FZPT	*Freiburger Zeitschrift für Philosophie und Theologie.*
HAT	Handbuch zum Alten Testament.
IB	Interpreter's Bible.
ICC	International Critical Commentary.
JBL	*Journal of Biblical Literature.*
JNES	*Journal of Near Eastern Studies.*
JSOT	*Journal for the Study of the Old Testament.*
JTS	*Journal of Theological Studies.*
KAT	Kommentar zum Alten Testament.
KHAT	Kurzer Hand-Commentar zum Alten Testament.
LXX	The Septuagint.

MT	The Massoretic Text.
NEB	New English Bible.
NICOT	New International Commentary on the Old Testament.
OAN	Oracles against the nations.
OTL	Old Testament Library.
OTS	*Oudtestamentische Studien.*
RB	*Revue Biblique.*
RSV	Revised Standard Version, 1971.
SBL	Society of Biblical Literature.
SVT	*Supplements to Vetus Testamentum.*
TynB	*Tyndale Bulletin.*
VSH	*Vanderbildt Studies in the Humanities.*
VT	*Vetus Testamentum.*
WMANT	Wissenschaftliche Monographien zum Alten und Neuen Testament.
ZAW	*Zeitschrift für die alttestamentliche Wissenschaft.*
ZTK	*Zeitschrift für Theologie und Kirche.*

Note

In this volume the book of Jeremiah is referred to as *Jeremiah* (in italics) to avoid ambiguity.

Introduction

The present volume is a study of the book of *Jeremiah* which aims to elucidate its purpose and theology in dialogue with the widely held belief that it is a product of Deuteronomistic editing. To state our aim thus is to rest the emphasis squarely on *Jeremiah*, and allow the reader to hope for clarification (above all) of what is especially interesting and important in that book. At the same time, it reveals one of the central contentions of the study, namely that the characterization of *Jeremiah* as Deuteronomistic obscures its individuality and vitality, and retards rather than furthers the task of its elucidation.

If this opening gambit seems headstrong, it does not imply, I hope, a disregard for the difficulty of the questions which surround any attempt to account for *Jeremiah* as a phenomenon, or for the many attempts to do so which have come to solutions other than the one which I want to propose. On the contrary, the quest for some plausible setting for the book is indispensable to its meaning, and that quest is not straightforward on any account of the matter. Whether one views this huge book as a composition which owes much to exilic and post-exilic editing or finds it probable that much of it derives from the prophet Jeremiah himself, the need to explain its origin and formation as a book is inescapable.

The true proportions of the task of understanding *Jeremiah* begin to be seen, in fact, only when it is realized that it impinges on other major areas of Old Testament study – of which the charting of Israelite religion from the late pre-exilic to the early post-exilic period, the history of prophecy

11

and the composition and setting of the Deuteronomistic History (*i.e.* Deuteronomy – Kings, or DtH) are perhaps the most important. The study of *Jeremiah* does not merely draw from each of these, but also gives to them. Thus N. P. Lemche, in his methodological statement about the use of Old Testament literature as the raw material of historical study,[1] can cite *Jeremiah* along with DtH as a parade example of the need to distinguish between original prophetic utterance and later redaction. And R. P. Carroll's understanding of the growth of the book (that it owes much to a process of highly complex editing stretching well into the post-exilic period)[2] finds itself on cordial terms with G. Garbini's radical appraisal of the biblical presentation of history, as so ideologically motivated as to carry very little evidence at all of Israel's history.[3] The question of the setting and purpose of *Jeremiah* therefore, has implications which reach beyond the book itself.

The answers to the problem of *Jeremiah* are various. I do not propose to give a systematic account of them here, mainly because such accounts exist in accessible places,[4] but also because there is a lively contemporary debate about *Jeremiah* with which it is more urgent to interact. It involves two main approaches, which are hardly new in themselves, but they are broad and embrace contributions which are different from each other in important ways.

Jeremiah as a 'Deuteronomistic' production

The first approach is that which we referred to in the opening paragraph, embracing those treatments of *Jeremiah* which in some sense regard it as containing Deuteronomistic material or as the result of Deuteronomistic editing. In classifying all of these together it is important not to over-simplify. The seminal work was that of B. Duhm, who separated authentic words of Jeremiah from later Deuteronomistic accretions, leaning heavily on his belief that only poetic oracles could be genuine.[5] In his wake, S.

12

Mowinckel identified Jeremiah's prose sermons as a separate 'source' (his source 'C'),[6] which reflected the interests of the Deuteronomistic editors of DtH. Since this development, the idea of a Deuteronomistic presence in *Jeremiah* has ramified. One version is best known in the work of E. W. Nicholson, who regards the prose sermons as the deposit of preaching to the Babylonian exiles, in broad dependence on the work of the prophet but applying his thought to the urgent needs of ever new situations.[7] This view is similar to that of E. Janssen, with the significant difference that the latter located the preaching in the emergent Palestinian synagogue of the exilic period.[8]

Another version of the Deuteronomistic approach is that which was made current by J. P. Hyatt, and developed by W. Thiel, which sees *Jeremiah* essentially as a Deuteronomistic edition of the prophet's work.[9] This understanding has the advantage that it offers an account of the formation of the complete book.

Finally, the recent publications of R. P. Carroll and W. McKane may be mentioned in the broad category. Though they are not alike in all respects, they share a view which distinguishes them somewhat from all the above, namely, that *Jeremiah* is too diverse a creation to be subsumed under some comprehensive theory of setting or purpose. Thus McKane offers his idea of a 'rolling corpus', meaning that existing passages were reinterpreted, not according to any overarching editorial plan, but rather haphazardly, in response to ever new situations.[10] Carroll likewise eschews the overarching scheme, and looks to a variety of post-exilic settings to explain the host of essentially disparate pieces which he thinks compose the book.[11]

Despite the differences, however, the authors named have in common their belief that it is useful to apply the term 'Deuteronomistic' to *Jeremiah*, with the implication that the analogy thus invoked with other literature, specifically DtH, is illuminating. It is this point which, in my view, requires fresh examination.

Jeremiah as a work of the prophet

The alternative to the set of approaches which we have gathered under the label 'Deuteronomistic' is to attribute much or all of the book to the activity of Jeremiah himself. This view of *Jeremiah* also claims a solid pedigree within modern critical discussion, with important figures such as Th. Robinson and O. Eissfeldt associating the prose closely with the life and work of Jeremiah.[12] J. Bright's attempt to show the independence of the diction of the prose *vis-à-vis* that of DtH, and similarities between it and the poetry, thus establishing its authenticity to Jeremiah, is still a reference point in research.[13] And H. Weippert's contextual study of the prose speeches, with a similar aim, is an important extension of Bright's argument.[14]

The massive commentary of Holladay, bringing to a culmination decades of his own contributions on *Jeremiah*, is a recent major addition to the literature which attributes much of *Jeremiah* to the prophet. The special interest of Holladay's treatment is his attempt to account for the growth and promulgation of the book. He is not content, in other words, with a simplistic attribution of the book to Jeremiah, but takes seriously the need to relate prophet and prophecy. The composition of the book proceeds by the making of several scrolls, in which the role of Baruch, Jeremiah's amanuensis, is important, and which receives particular stimuli from the septennial readings of Deuteronomy at the Feast of Tabernacles (Dt. 31:10–11), which Holladay assumed to have happened in 622 BC, under the influence of Josiah's reform, and subsequently at seven-year intervals.[15]

The variety of utterances of Jeremiah, which is so important in the contrasting approach of Carroll and McKane, is explained in terms of a development in the theology of the prophet according to changing circumstances. Accordingly, Jeremiah at first hoped that the people of Judah, and even of the former northern kingdom, would repent and thus avert coming judgment. Later, however, he embraced a theology, whose essence is expressed in the 'new covenant', in which

14

the judgment of exile becomes unavoidable, and in which a new salvation is expected through a redeeming act of YHWH.[16] A somewhat similar view of changes in Jeremiah's message was adopted by T. M. Raitt, and this has found echoes in the recent work of J. Unterman.[17] Holladay's most significant achievement, however, is that he has engaged with the Deuteronomistic interpretation at the crucial point of offering an account of the formation of the book.

These, then, are the two main claimants to interpret *Jeremiah*, the one focusing on the prophet himself, the other on a tradition more or less loosely associated with him. All that needs to be added is that the whole picture of recent study of *Jeremiah* is not one of clean polarization. Rather, certain studies, though they have a high estimate of Jeremiah's contribution to the book, nevertheless also allow a degree of subsequent development. J. A. Thompson is one such commentator.[18] R. R. Wilson too, in his work on the social location of prophets, finds it difficult, as we shall see at a later stage, to identify a clear boundary between the speech of the prophet himself and that of the group which surrounded and supported him.[19]

Having entered this caveat, we can nevertheless conclude that the main lines of interpretation follow well-established paths, traceable on the one hand to Duhm, and on the other (within the parameters of modern criticism) perhaps to Robinson and Eissfeldt. The tenacity of both approaches testifies, no doubt, to the difficulty of deriving unambiguous evidence from the material. It is all the more important, therefore, to give some attention to the criteria which lead scholars to their different decisions.

Criteria for determining the setting and purpose of *Jeremiah*

The two main criteria, by which scholars have judged *Jeremiah* to be Deuteronomistic or otherwise, are stylistic and theological. We shall consider the former first.

a. Style

The style of the prose speeches has been a prominent factor in 'Deuteronomistic' interpretations of *Jeremiah*. The contention that prophets typically spoke in poetry, together with the observation that the prose speeches of Jeremiah resembled that of speeches in DtH, gave potency to Mowinckel's thesis. The feeling was strong that the hand of the Deuteronomist was conspicuous, being not merely prosaic, but also banal. Terms such as 'moralistic', 'legalistic', 'dogmatic', 'monotonous' and 'impoverished' were the common coin of Deuteronomistic interpretations.[20] Clearly, evaluations such as these were aimed at deficiencies not only of style but also of thought. The stylistic criterion itself, however, was taken further by Janssen, who considered not only vocabulary, but found a common speech-form in *Jeremiah* and DtH. His location of the speeches in the Palestinian synagogue was essentially a form-critical argument.[21]

Today, however, the style criterion looks much less secure than it did to Duhm and Mowinckel. The reason is that the issue is not the mere identification of a style, or even of a set of ideas typically couched in certain terms, but the need for a reliable control on the origin of such diction, and this is elusive. The point is a logical one. Merely to observe similarities between the diction of two bodies of literature says nothing about the origin of the kind of expression that is common to both. For this reason, an earlier generation of scholars could think that Jeremiah wrote Deuteronomy.[22] And R. E. Friedman has recently given a new twist to the idea with his view that Jeremiah wrote not only *Jeremiah* but DtH as well.[23] The argument about similarity, it seems, can cut either way when it comes to dependence. It can also become circular. Even Janssen's rather sophisticated form-critical argument, for example, illustrates the point, when it makes the *Jeremiah* prose a major factor in producing the theory of the incipient Palestinian synagogue, which in turn explains the prose. The argument from style, in short, leads to a logical impasse.

16

By the same token, lexicographical descriptions of the sermons of *Jeremiah* and DtH designed to show the independence of the former have met with serious criticism. H. Weippert made the point against Bright that his methodology relied too heavily on statistical evidence about words and phrases, rather than on whole contexts. Appealing to Saussurean principles, she concentrated, not on words and phrases in themselves (*parole*), but on their use in context (*language*). Her conclusion, that analogies existed between the diction of the prose and the poetry, was intended to strengthen the case for the independence of Jeremiah.[24]

Weippert herself, however, has not avoided the kinds of strictures which she herself levelled at Bright. While acknowledging her real progress in the attempt to show the *significance* of lexicographical observations, McKane rightly concludes that she has not proved the provenance of the prose from Jeremiah. This is because, for all her interest in contexts, those with which she works are still discrete; that is, they provide no account of the discourse in a sustained way. McKane is finally unpersuaded, because she offers no explanation of what he sees as the 'complicated, untidy accumulation of material' that comprises *Jeremiah* 1–25.[25] McKane thus points to the necessity of interpreting the parts of the discourse ultimately in the context of the largest literary blocks to which they belong. The point is crucially important, and we shall return to it.

The use of the criterion of style, finally, has undergone important changes in some recent studies. Thiel identifies the Deuteronomist (or D.) in *Jeremiah* not only on the basis of stylistic parallels with other Deuteronomistic writing, but from an understanding of the style of the D. in *Jeremiah* built up entirely on arguments internal to the book. This is a new kind of circularity in the 'Deuteronomistic' interpretation of *Jeremiah*, characterized by McKane as 'heads I win and tails you lose'.[26] In Carroll, by contrast, the criterion is not very significant, as the idea of 'authentic' words of Jeremiah retreats almost from sight, and the whole portrayal of the prophet, poetry and prose, is a product of Deuteronomistic activity.[27]

The criterion of style, therefore, has been used in widely various ways. Frequently, too much weight has been attached to stylistic arguments, of whatever kind, and the only sensible conclusion is that we cannot conclude much from it, either about the authenticity of the prose or about its origin in a Deuteronomistic movement. It is quite possible, in fact, that the relationship between the prose of *Jeremiah* and that of DtH is complex. Thus, as we shall argue in a later chapter, it is likely that the author of *Jeremiah* 36 is influenced, in a very special sense, by the narrative of 2 Kings 22.[28] But this does not force the conclusion that all stylistic similarities between the two corpora are to be explained by the dependence of *Jeremiah* on DtH. To observe similarities is one matter; to decide their significance is another. They may, indeed, be a function of quite complex social, religious and literary relationships. It follows that the origin of the *Jeremiah* prose, and its relation to the poetry, must be decided primarily on other sorts of grounds.

b. Theology

It was apparent in our survey of style in the assessment of the *Jeremiah* prose that it was impossible to separate this criterion from that of theology. Not only were the speeches held to lack sparkle but their thought was shallow and legalistic, in this also resembling DtH. The editor of *Jeremiah*, according to Hyatt, aimed to show how Jeremiah '... was in general agreement with the ideas and purposes of the Deuteronomic school'.[29] That is, the speeches aimed to depict him as a supporter of Josiah's reform, who argued that the exile had come as a result of disobedience to the Mosaic law, and that future hope for the nation depended on renewed obedience to it. A classic text was *Jeremiah* 11:1–16, which, with its many echoes of the language and thought of Deuteronomy,[30] was seen as the Deuteronomist's attempt to make Jeremiah a mouthpiece of the reform.

It is clear that there are indeed similarities between

Deuteronomy, DtH and the *Jeremiah* prose, which go beyond the merely stylistic. They share a covenantal theology in which themes of covenant faithfulness and land-possession are prominent. But it does not follow from this observation that they are in all respects similar, or that they have identical purposes. Indeed, the rather negative value-judgments passed upon these corpora often fail to perceive not only that the theologies of each have some subtlety, but that they are also individual. This rather different value-judgment is supported by a number of recent studies of various parts of the Deuteronomistic literature and of *Jeremiah*.[31] And it seems to me that, inasmuch as the style and theology of *Jeremiah*, as well as of Deuteronomy and DtH, are investigated in relatively large literary contexts, more positive and differentiated assessments of them will be made.

Indeed, when we begin to consider the *Jeremiah* prose on a broader canvas, and in the context of the whole book, it becomes apparent that serious problems attach to the view that Jeremiah is presented as a mouthpiece of the Josianic reform. First, Jeremiah is scarcely depicted as a believer in the need to centralize the worship of Israel in the Jerusalem temple. At two prominent points in the book (though the reference may be to a single event) he boldly castigates the practices there (7:1–15; 26:1–6). Second, there is no explicit statement of his support for the reform. The problem arising from the fact that his call to prophesy is dated after the beginning of the reform,[32] and that he is said to have prophesied continuously for twenty-three years up to the fourth year of Jehoiakim (605 BC), with only scant praise at that for King Josiah, has long been recognized.[33] Conversely, there is no mention of Jeremiah in Kings, though like *Jeremiah* it covers the period up to the exile. This mutual coolness towards the two major figures in the respective works, though they treat the same theme and the same period, gives pause to the supposition that they emanate from similar or identical circles.

These observations, however, do not take us to the heart of the matter. The fact is that *Jeremiah* and DtH express hope

19

for the future of Israel in quite different ways. The point raises the complex question of how *Jeremiah* relates on the one hand to earlier prophets, and on the other to Deuteronomy, and this matter will have to be taken up in its own right at a later stage. At this point, however, we can observe that *Jeremiah*'s hope stands closer to both Deuteronomy 30:1–10 and Hosea than to DtH. This is because, of the four blocks of material in question (Dt. 30:1–10; Hosea;[34] *Jeremiah* and DtH), only DtH refrains from holding out a hope of return to the historic promised land following the exile. The other three do so explicitly. In *Jeremiah*, indeed, it is the dominant theme of the great central section of the book known as the 'Book of Consolation', because it articulates new promises of salvation in ways that contrast sharply and gloriously with the images of judgment which form the substance of much of the first half of the book. The salvation theology in question, moreover, is not distinguished by its promise of a return to the land alone. It has also frequently been referred to as *redemption* theology, because it goes beyond the call to repentance (which characterizes DtH, and no doubt also much of Jeremiah's actual early preaching) to assert that hope for the future reposes in the readiness of YHWH himself to take a new initiative in forging a satisfactory covenantal relationship with his people. This theology, it should be stressed, is not unique to *Jeremiah*. If *Jeremiah* develops it beyond Deuteronomy and Hosea, it nevertheless does so in terms which are reminiscent of those two books.[35]

The question of hope in DtH is, it must be said, a complex one in its own right. According to one influential theory of its composition (that of Cross), an earlier edition of DtH than the one which we now possess, originating as a programme for Josiah's reform, expected Israel's continued existence in the land without an exile at all.[36] Some have argued, furthermore, that the release of the exiled King Jehoiachin from his Babylonian prison (2 Ki. 25:27–30) was seen by the author of DtH as a chink of hope for the future.[37] In my view, however, neither of these interpretations correctly understands the view of DtH on the future of Israel. The latest trend in studies of DtH, or at least of Kings, it seems to me, is towards a return to Noth's view of a single author.[38] I myself have argued elsewhere for a unifying concept in the books of Kings, challenging the view that there was ever an edition of DtH which set hopes on the historic Davidic monarchy.[39] The point will be taken up at a later stage in a comparison of Jehoiakim's reception of Jeremiah's words (Je. 36) with Josiah's openness to the newly discovered 'book of the law' (2 Ki. 22).[40]

As for other tell-tale signs of DtH's prospect on the future, none is more illuminating than the prayer of Solomon in 1 Kings 8:46–53. This is the passage which, more than any other in DtH, speaks of a renewed relationship between God and Israel after the judgment of exile has befallen the people. And the prayer conspicuously omits any mention of return to the land.[41]

It follows that very considerable differences of perspective exist between *Jeremiah* and DtH on what must have been the crucial issue for the people at the time of the exile, namely, what kind of future they could expect following the apparent lapse of the covenant relationship. Of course, the observations we have made raise an extremely important issue of principle. That is, how far may perceptible tendencies in any large literary corpus be taken to be representative of the whole? Do any of the corpora in question possess a unity of conception, or are they not rather composed of diverse strands, possibly exhibiting more than one point of view on important issues?

Some of the features we have noticed suggest that there are indeed considered and *consistent* differences between *Jeremiah* and DtH (*e.g.* the attitude to Josiah and the reform in *Jeremiah*; the absence of any allusion to Jeremiah in DtH; the distancing from Dt. 30:1–10 in 1 Ki. 8:46–53). On the other hand, all the 'Deuteronomistic' treatments of *Jeremiah* face the problem that 'Deuteronomistic' has to be specially defined for the prophetic book. Nicholson, for example, explains *Jeremiah*'s redemption theology as a development within the Deuteronomistic kerygma.[42] On this view, calls to

21

repent in *Jeremiah* (such as 18:7–10) stand cheek by jowl with the redemption theology just described (*e.g.* in 24:7), and the latter sort is seen as a development within the tradition. This, however, raises the question whether it remains useful to regard the relevant *Jeremiah* material as Deuteronomistic. The problem for the Deuteronomistic approach is evident in some of the statements of Carroll, who is driven by the differences between *Jeremiah* and DtH to the suggestion: 'Perhaps within Deuteronomistic circles there were those who worked specifically on a production of Jeremiah.'[43] Arguments of this sort illustrate the difficulty of describing *Jeremiah* as a production of Deuteronomistic circles. Attempts to do so run up against the individuality of *Jeremiah*, and the subsumption of *Jeremiah*'s individual features under the broad rubric 'Deuteronomistic' lacks external controls.[44]

One further point needs to be made by way of caveat, however. That is, it is possible to over-react to the 'Deuteronomistic' interpretation of *Jeremiah* by insisting too strongly on the differences between *Jeremiah* on the one hand and Deuteronomy and DtH on the other. This tendency in the work of Weippert has been criticized, rightly I think, by McKane,[45] on the grounds that it puts too much weight on fine semantic differences. In fact, the relationship among Deuteronomy, the prophetic tradition, DtH and *Jeremiah* is a complex one, and *Jeremiah* has features in common with them all, as we shall see at various points in the argument.

Approaching *Jeremiah*: the part and the whole

The issue of principle which I want to raise in the present study is whether a reading of *Jeremiah* should begin, as it were, with the small component, and work out towards the whole composition, or rather with the whole, in whose context the disparate parts should ultimately be evaluated and understood. The 'Deuteronomistic' interpretation, I believe, is necessarily pursued by means of a piecemeal approach to the text. Small units are compared first of all with other units, in

Jeremiah or beyond, which exhibit similar characteristics, and so a picture of a Deuteronomistic redaction is built up. The piecemeal approach and the 'Deuteronomistic' interpretation belong together *ex hypothesi*. In Carroll's work in particular, the profusion of multiplied entities is not always matched by the plausibility of the suggested settings.

My reading of *Jeremiah*, in contrast, depends on seeing the component parts of *Jeremiah* first of all in their literary relationships within the book. Thus, the meaning of 18:7–10 (to take a passage that has already been mentioned) emerges only from a reading of the account of Jeremiah's first visit to the potter (18:1–11) together with the account of his second (19:1–15).[46] The text is therefore seen, in its finished form, as a kind of reflection upon its parts. This approach requires that the book is the product of careful and sophisticated editing, substantially the work, as I believe, of one mind.

For this reason I find myself in constant disagreement with the approaches of McKane and Carroll, who, in their own ways, have stressed the disparate character and the editorial complexity of *Jeremiah*. In one sense, it must be agreed that the work is complex. Complexity is perfectly consistent with its being the deposit of the approximately forty-year ministry of Jeremiah. The process of the material's growth, moreover, is difficult or impossible (*pace* Holladay) to trace, and no attempt is made to do so here. The particular views of *Jeremiah*'s complexity taken by Carroll and McKane, however, are not required, I think, by the nature of the material, but only by the methods they have chosen. It is important to say at this stage that this is the nature of my disagreement with them. The alternative approach taken here manifests itself, inevitably, at almost every point in the argument. Yet my purpose is not a point by point critique. The difference lies in the starting-point. Furthermore, the argument cannot be won or lost by the swapping of readings of individual texts, nor, or course, by the mere appeal to complexity. The approaches must be evaluated whole, for their power to account for the material in its present form.

The method

Our method will be to consider the various sections of the completed book (MT), in sequence and in relation to each other. The aim is to try to see whether there is a rationale for the inclusion in one corpus of so much disparate material. The disparities between various components of the book, when removed from their immediate contexts and juxtaposed, have been a major plank in the platform of all those who think the book has grown somewhat haphazardly and now contains the diverse views of different groups in exilic and post-exilic Judah. (The Temple sermon, for example, Je. 7:1–15, is ill at ease with the promise of renewed permanent institutions in Je. 33:14–26 when the two are simply placed side by side.)[47] Whether such juxtapositions really force the conclusion that *Jeremiah* is a haphazard compilation is a theory which requires to be tested, I believe, by a study of large contexts, and ultimately the book as a whole.[48] Is there a rationale for the whole book which enables us to see the relationships among the parts differently?

The thesis will be that there is indeed such a rationale, and that it centres on the theology which comes to its fullest expression in the 'Book of Consolation', though it is contained in other important passages such as *Jeremiah* 24. This theology is arrived at as a result of Jeremiah's reflection on his own message throughout his ministry, as well as on Deuteronomy, the prophetic tradition (especially Hosea, but not exclusively so), and on parts at least of DtH. The mature Jeremiah knows that Judah could not have avoided the exile because of her inability to be other than apostate. He sees the exile as a necessary purifying judgment, and holds out hope of a wholly new kind of covenantal arrangement, in which the people will be enabled to live in harmony with YHWH in the ancient land.

The book of *Jeremiah* is a redaction. That is to say, what we may take to have been early statements of Jeremiah have been given new meanings, both in the light of experience, and by the activity of collecting and shaping various sayings

24

and records of the prophet's actions into the literary creation which we now possess. We may suppose that Baruch, or even others, played some role alongside Jeremiah in this. It may be also that the work was not done all at once, and that this partly explains why two rather different textual traditions (MT and LXX) appear to have existed independently from a relatively early period.[49]

The point about new contexts producing new meanings for original sayings is an important one. In this sense the present study resembles certain 'Deuteronomistic' interpretations, and is *un*like others which propose that the prophet made a large contribution to the formation of the book. The point is illustrated by a comparison between the present study and the works of T. M. Raitt and J. Unterman.[50] While it has important elements in common with these (especially with the latter) I do not see *Jeremiah* as evidence of the prophet's changing message in quite the same way as they do, *i.e.* where certain texts are taken as evidence of an early 'repentance' theology, and others of the 'redemption' theology which in due course superseded it.[51] Rather, the relationship between repentance and redemption is a theological topic of the book, and indeed reflection on it is one of the important characteristics of the final redaction. The point will be illustrated in our discussion of the calls to repentance in *Jeremiah* 3:1 – 4:4 (see below, chapter 1).

The same perception, indeed, informs our study of the book at a higher level of organization also. We shall proceed, first, with a study of *Jeremiah* 1 – 24. Obviously, within the confines of a volume of this sort, we cannot be exhaustive in this. Rather, we shall try to show how the organization of the material testifies to the abandonment of hope that the exile might be averted by repentance. A chapter on the so-called Confessions of Jeremiah shows how reflection on the role of the prophet serves the basic theme of this part of the book. There follows a consideration of chapters 25 – 45 (prefaced by a brief analysis of the structure of those chapters), which express the revival of hope, now understood in a new way. Once again attention is given to the role of the prophet, and how it is related to the theme of this second major section of the book. The oracles against the nations (chapters 46 – 51), incidentally a specifically prophetic phenomenon, are then shown to be integrated into the argument of the whole book. Finally, in the light of our appreciation of the theology of *Jeremiah*, we shall consider in what way it might be considered to belong authentically within the Israelite prophetic tradition.

CHAPTER ONE

Repentance and hope (3:1 – 4:4)

We have now looked critically at attempts to relate the parts of the book of *Jeremiah* to the life of the prophet or to other historical periods. Such attempts were invariably made in the context of some broader view of the way in which prophetic books were composed, as the contrasting approaches of Holladay and Carroll well illustrate.

The problem of relating the book to the prophet is inevitably posed in our own study. The question of the setting, not only of the book but of its parts, is perplexing, both for those who look for settings in the life of the prophet and for those who look elsewhere. While I shall ultimately argue for a setting in the life of the prophet, I take the view that not many of the poetic oracles in particular can be dated with much accuracy. Nor is it always possible to be confident about the beginnings and endings of individual sayings. The thesis I propose is that the great variety within the book, including variety of theological viewpoint in relation to themes, is explicable in terms of the long ministry of the prophet, in which his message varied according to the people's reaction to it. There is a sense, then, in which all that Jeremiah ever said is mediated to readers of the book through a retrospect. The individual parts which make up the book have become part of a whole which has, obviously, taken its shape after the exile of Judah to Babylon. Therefore, even where we can successfully identify original oracles of the prophet, we have not thereby merely recovered a set of disparate sayings. Rather, we see something of the way in which those sayings were regarded in the light of experience (of judgment come), and through the eyes of the compiler of the book. For this reason the book itself does not generally invite us to reconstruct its constituent parts, and therefore we are hard put to it to do so.

The difficulty we face, therefore, is that the variety within the book, including theological variety, is explicable, I believe, in terms of the changing scenes of Jeremiah's life, yet the book by its nature does not permit us to reconstruct those changes with much thoroughness. The point may be illustrated by posing the question: did Jeremiah ever hold out hope that Judah (or perhaps a residue of northern Israel) might actually repent and therefore avoid the judgment with which YHWH was threatening them? If he did, how may such a message function in the context of a book which knows that in fact the people did not repent, and judgment did come? The question is important, incidentally, for the comparison between the theology of *Jeremiah* and DtH, as we shall see. In the present chapter, however, we shall focus on *Jeremiah* 3:1 – 4:4, which features the most sustained thinking about repentance in the book.

It is important at the outset, however, to observe that this passage is itself part of the longer section which begins at 2:1 and ends at 4:4. Its dominant theme is Judah's apostasy, depicted in rich metaphors in chapter 2. We are interested primarily in 3:1 – 4:4 because it is there that the theme of 'repentance', or 'return' (the verb is *šûb*), is developed. The repentance theme of chapter 3, however, belongs closely with that of apostasy in chapter 2. In connection with both of these themes, it is important to establish what is meant by the terms 'Israel' and 'Judah', which occur several times in both chapters. Our understanding of what Jeremiah meant by repentance will depend on this. Does chapter 3 contain a memory of an early appeal by the prophet to the people of 'Israel', in the sense of the former northern kingdom? Or does 'Israel' refer more generally to the covenant people, now represented by Judah alone? As we try to answer these questions we shall also see something of how chapter 3, as it stands, represents a reshaping of what Jeremiah may originally have said, in accordance with his developing message.

'Israel' in *Jeremiah* 2

In chapter 2, the name Israel is used as well as Judah (3f., 14, 26). Indeed, the rehearsal of the salvation history which is the context of the accusation of the people is in terms of the historic Israel. Thus, the introductory reminiscence in verses 3f. evokes the wilderness period, when Israel as a unity entered into relationship with YHWH. This use of the name to recall historic Israel predominates in the chapter, and lies behind the terms of the accusation in general (*e.g.* 6f., 21, *cf.* Ps. 80:8). Such a use of the name implies that the Judah that is addressed by Jeremiah can be seen as an embodiment of the historic people, and that indeed is one of the burdens of the chapter.

There are some indications, however, that the use of the name is more complex than this. In verse 4, the phrase 'O house of Jacob, and all the families of the house of Israel' refers to the nation in a way which distinguishes its parts. Commentators have sought to explain this usage in various ways. Some see it as a natural extension of the use of the name Israel described in the last paragraph. Thus Thompson thinks it natural enough that in the context of some covenant festival Judah should be addressed as 'representing "all the tribes of the house of Israel"', a view which is close to Carroll's.[1] McKane too believes the expression is an archaism designed to embrace all the generations of Israel in the accusation that follows.[2] Holladay, on the other hand, finds evidence in the phrase in question for his theory of a first rescension of Jeremiah's words in chapter 2 which was addressed to the former northern kingdom just before the death of Josiah in 609 BC.[3] Holladay is not alone in finding evidence of an early ministry of Jeremiah in the north, connected with Josiah's expansion there, and the weakening of Assyrian power.[4] If such views fall short of proof, part of their strength is in the present phraseology, which seems to go beyond the mere identification of historic Israel with contemporary Judah.

A further passage which suggests the thought of Israel as

the northern kingdom is verses 26–28, which begins with 'Israel' (26), and ends with 'Judah' (28). Commentators generally interpret the passage as a simple equation of the two entities.[5] The equation is given further credence by translations (as RSV) which render verse 26b, 'the house of Israel shall be shamed'. The future tense is in fact gratuitous, and most commentators translate with either a present[6] or a past tense.[7] Verse 26 aims, in fact, to convey the shame of past sin, up to the present. In this way it is in line with the thrust of the chapter, which stresses continuity between past and present apostasy. The movement from 'Israel' to 'Judah', however, may carry the additional suggestion of a comparison between the former northern kingdom and present Judah. The change of focus comes in the very last word of verse 28, and in the context has the force of a surprise.

A final consideration regarding the identity of Israel in chapter 2 is the meaning of allusions to Assyria. These come explicitly in verses 18 and 36, and implicitly in verses 14f., which speak of a past enslavement. But who is Assyria in these passages? There are in essence two possibilities. According to the first, the reference could be to the former Empire, now in decline, but which had destroyed the northern kingdom in 722 BC, and subsequently reduced Judah also (2 Ki. 18:9–16). On this reading, verse 36 is intelligible as a warning to Judah not to put trust in a political alliance with Egypt because past experience of a great power, on the part of both Israel and Judah, had been so disastrous. Verses 14f. are also comprehensible on this view, where the roaring of the lions (a sign of a kill completed) would be the victory song of Assyria in the era of Hoshea and Hezekiah. This is in fact Rudolph's understanding of these verses (though he sees 36f. as having a different setting and significance).[8] The line of thought would thus continue: Egypt has also proven a false hope;[9] what then can you, Judah, expect to gain by trusting in political alliances, either with Assyria or with Egypt (16–18)? Past disappointments are thus made the measure of the folly of present hopes. The plausibility of an

Egyptian alliance in Jeremiah's early period needs no special argument; and an arrangement with Assyria might seem attractive up to that Empire's final defeat by Babylon in 612 BC.

The second possible understanding of Assyria in the chapter is that its name is used much more in connection with contemporary events in Judah. There are variations of this view. For Carroll, the pairing of Assyria and Egypt is merely conventional and rhetorical, and therefore the language used in verses 15–16 and 18 is so general as not to require the identification of particular historical events behind it.[10] If such events *were* to be identified, then they would be events datable within the period of Jeremiah's ministry, and the 'Israel' of verse 14 is 'most definitely Judah'.[11] Holladay too interprets the passage in terms of events in Jeremiah's time, and sees Assyria as a cipher for Babylon.[12] The advantages of this position are that the 'lion' metaphor in 4:7 is usually understood of Babylon, and may therefore be so understood by analogy in verse 15. Assyria is certainly used in a similar way, furthermore, in at least one other place in the Old Testament (*viz.* Ezr. 6:22, where it means Persia). Verses 14f., therefore, are set by both Holladay and Carroll in the period of Babylonian ascendancy; the conventional terms 'Israel' and 'Assyria' only lightly veil the true referents, namely Judah and Babylon.

This latter position, however, disposes too lightly of Israel's history with Assyria. The argument based on the 'lions' metaphor and analogy with 4:7 is inconclusive because the referent might easily shift between one occurrence and another; indeed such a shift may well be intended and help create the meaning of the later use of the metaphor. (The same metaphor is, incidentally, used for Assyria in Is. 5:29; Am. 3:12.) The first position outlined above produces a more effective argument. It is the actual memory of past discomfiture through falsely placed trust in Empire which gives force to the warning not to make the same mistake again. Such a warning characterizes the arguments both of verses 14–18 and verse 36. Jeremiah is thus in a prophetic

31

tradition of argument, and particularly in line with Isaiah's opposition to an Assyrian alliance.[13]

It follows (*pace* Carroll) that when Jeremiah says Assyria and Israel, he means, in the first instance, Assyria and Israel. Carroll, in fact, is quite misleading when he supposes that a poetic, rhetorical reading of the passage stands over against a historical reading.[14] The contrary is the case; the rhetoric would be meaningless without a consciousness of the events in the background. This explains why Assyria can become a kind of cipher (as in Ezr. 6:22). Assyria is a paradigm of Empire as oppressor, of hopes that are doomed to disappointment because of the inalienably self-serving character of the overlord. Holladay, therefore, is not wrong to say that '"Assyria" here really means Babylon'.[15] In an important sense this is true. The reference to the river (18), for example, subtly turns the thought from Assyria (whose capital Nineveh stood on the Tigris), to Babylon, because 'the river' normally refers to the Euphrates (hence RSV *etc.*). Yet it does not follow that Assyria simply stands for Babylon in such a way as to extinguish all thought of the former. Rather, the thought moves from the one to the other. (The allusion to 'the river' actually facilitates this, being essentially ambiguous; it does on one occasion refer to the Tigris, Dn. 10:4.)[16] The historical Assyria gives point to the analogy.

We can now make a judgment about the meaning of Israel in verses 15–18 and 36. If Jeremiah recalls the actual depredations of Assyria, then he is also recalling those which were perpetrated against the northern kingdom (at least alongside the sufferings of Judah at the same hands). The fate of the northern kingdom, therefore, is recalled precisely for the benefit of contemporary Judah. The point can be made by considering the meaning of verse 36b:

> 'You shall be put to shame by Egypt
> as you were put to shame by Assyria.'

The best interpretation of the couplet is that, as the northern kingdom was disappointed in its trust in Assyria, so Judah will be disappointed in its trust in Egypt. The thought is complex. Israel in the sense of the northern kingdom is not wholly distinct from Israel in the sense of the historic people, the people now represented by Judah. In fact the couplet portrays both Israel and Judah as separate entities, and the two together as representing historic Israel. The verse shows well how elusive the idea of Israel is in the rhetoric of the chapter. Similar shifts and ambiguities in the use of the term can be found elsewhere in the Old Testament.[17]

Interpretation of 3:1 – 4:4

The interpretation of the names 'Israel' and 'Judah' in *Jeremiah* 2 was an important prelude to our consideration of *Jeremiah* 3 because discussions of the meaning and unity of the latter chapter focus in some measure upon it. This is because it is often said that 3:6–11 mistakenly suppose 3:1–5, with verses 12f., to have been spoken of the northern kingdom. McKane and Carroll represent this view. McKane writes: 'there is no reason to suppose that vv. 1–5 relate so particularly to the former northern kingdom'.[18] Carroll speaks of a failure to understand that '"Israel" in the discourse [by which he means the body of chapter 2 and 3:1–5] refers to Judah'.[19] Both, therefore, regard verses 6–11 as a misguided piece of interpretation. Their understanding of the meaning of 'Israel' in the chapter, therefore, undergirds their belief that the chapter is a mosaic with no coherent meaning, and they look for settings in the Jewish community after the fall of Jerusalem for the theologizing which they find, for example, in verses 6–11.

We shall return to the views of McKane and Carroll shortly. First, however, we shall consider the meaning of 3:1 – 4:4 in the light of our observations so far.

The opening passage, 3:1–5, declares the impossibility of reconciliation between YHWH and Judah because of Judah's apostasy, by analogy with the irreconcilability of a husband and wife after their divorce and the wife's second marriage.

33

The oracle is thus based on the law of Deuteronomy 24:1–4. The meaning of the oracle is that, a separation having been made between YHWH and Judah, and Judah having sought other 'lovers' (3:1; *cf.* 2:33), there can be no expectation of reconciliation with YHWH. The strength of the point is the greater because of the known fate of the northern kingdom, which a century after its dispersal to parts of the Assyrian Empire had simply disappeared from history. This analogy between the fates of north and south has been prepared for in chapter 2.

The next section is 3:6–14. Strictly, these verses comprise two oracles, each with its own new beginning (6, 11). Nevertheless they belong together because of unity of theme. The first is dated to the reign of King Josiah (6).

Verses 6–11 develop the divorce metaphor from verses 1–5, by making the unrepaired breach between northern Israel and YHWH an explicit object lesson for Judah (8). There are clear continuities in thought and language from the previous verses, most obviously in the metaphor of harlotry. Here too, the divorce idea raises the question of the possibility of a restored relationship. In verses 1–5, it was put rhetorically, as an outrageous thought, confirmed as such by the falseness of the appeal to YHWH (4b–5a). Here, Israel's apostasy (that is, the northern kingdom's) is seen from a slightly different point of view, as a closed chapter. Her opportunity, and failure, to return are in the past (7). The definitive nature of the judgment on Israel is further emphasized by the phrase 'faithless Israel' (6, *cf.* 12, 14).

The train of thought thus outlined has its logical conclusion in its implications for Judah. Judah should have learned from Israel's experience, but did not (8, 10). The retrospective character of the comment on Israel is true also for Judah.

The second oracle begins at verse 11 with a word which builds on verses 6–10, but takes another slightly different tack. Verse 11 shares with the preceding verses the retrospective accusation of faithlessness on the part of both Israel and Judah. The new idea is that Judah is actually even worse than Israel had been. Verses 12–14 then make an appeal (which Jeremiah is to address 'to the north', 12) to Israel to return (or 'repent'). The expression 'faithless Israel' (12) both serves to forge a further link with the thought of verses 6–10 and, by means of the shift to 'faithless children' (14), allows the appeal to be addressed in reality to Judah. The function of the appeal to the north, therefore, is to elaborate the purpose of verse 11; it is rhetorical in character, bringing the comparison between Israel and Judah to bear on the latter.

The force of the comparison, of course, is ironic, suggesting Judah's inability to repent. This thrust of the argument is strengthened by the repeated use of the epithet 'faithless'. There is a certain despair in the appeal in verse 12 (repeated in 14): 'Return, faithless Israel ...'. The word 'faithless' is the word *mᵉšubâ*, related to *šûḇ* (repent, return, turn). The implication is that the call to repent is likely to be of little avail with a nation that is incurably fickle. Even if it turns to YHWH there is no guarantee that it will not 'turn back' to other gods. *Jeremiah* 3:19–20 picture precisely this *šûḇ* of Judah's away from YHWH. (The same thought, with similar phraseology, recurs in 8:4–6.)

At two points in chapter 3 this idea of Judah's inability to repent gives way to another idea, namely an intervention on the part of YHWH himself to alter the situation radically. The first is in verse 14b, with its promise of a work of redemption undertaken by YHWH himself, which will be further developed in verses 15–18. The second is in verses 22–24. Verse 22 opens with the phrase: *Šûḇû bānîm šôḇāḇîm; 'erpâ mᵉšûḇōthêkem*. Here we have the greatest concentration of play with the word *šûḇ*, which not only repeats the irony initiated in verse 12 but accepts the impasse entailed in calling to repentance those who cannot repent, and adumbrates what will become an essential part of the answer of *Jeremiah* to the problem of Judah's intransigence, namely a work of God himself in transcending that inherent inability in his people. We shall return to this aspect of the thought of the book in due course.

Did Jeremiah preach repentance?

At this point, however, we must face again the question with which we began the present enquiry, namely what kind of evidence does the present passage afford for a phase of Jeremiah's ministry in which he preached repentance with a hope or expectation that his hearers might obey? The question arises because of what we have just observed, that in the same breath in which the call to repent is made, the possibility of it seems to be denied. Are these verses, then, only retrospective theologizing, and no evidence for a real preaching of repentance?

There are three possible answers to the question: (a) that Jeremiah preached repentance to the northern kingdom in the days of Josiah; (b) that he preached repentance to Judah, and (c) that he did neither, but that the idea of such repentance preaching belongs to exilic or post-exilic theological debates. The first view is taken, for example, by Rudolph, who points to Jeremiah's own Benjaminite origins as the motive for his concern, and sees the call to 'return' as an invitation to come back to the 'homeland', now that the north's former sins have been purged by exile.[20] Bright and Holladay are broadly in line with Rudolph, though they see the original idea of a political return shading over into a call for return in reality to YHWH.[21]

There are real difficulties with this view. In the first place, it lacks *prima facie* plausibility. Against it stands the fact that the historic Israelite people of the north can scarcely have had a recognizable existence a century after the Assyrian policy had scattered them and brought other peoples to their former home. Josiah's symbolic reclamation of former Israelite territory, furthermore (2 Ki. 23), cannot be called in support of a ministry of Jeremiah to the north, in view of Jeremiah's resistance in general to alignment with Josiah's policies. The idea that the verb *šûb* when applied to the north means a literal return home is therefore fragile.

In fact, the meaning of *šûb* in the chapter is a serious difficulty for the view. Holladay's scenario illustrates the problem. He thinks the appeal to the north referred primarily to a geographical return from exile in Assyria, but that behind it lies a call to return to YHWH. This latter idea will have been uppermost in Jeremiah's mind when the call to 'return' was applied to Judah before the exile. But when Judah had herself experienced exile the word shifted in meaning once again to bear a connotation of geographical return.[22] It is unlikely that the present text is best explained by postulating this complicated sequence of events. It is unlikely too that the verb *šûḇ* was ever used merely of geographical return to the homeland. The present passage certainly offers no evidence to support such a view.

Leaving aside for the moment the second possible answer to the question whether Jeremiah preached repentance, we move to the third, namely Carroll's belief, mentioned above, that discussions relating to repentance and return to the land belong to post-exilic debate. These discussions, for him, bear not upon repentance and return in and of themselves, but upon the rights of rival groups within the restoration community. These groups are, on the one hand, the Palestinian group which did not go through the exile and, on the other, the returned exiles. The debate between them he regards as an important key to the understanding of the book as a whole. In the present passage he thinks the term 'Judah' signifies the post-exilic Palestinian community, while 'Israel' is used of the returned exiles. 'This comparative praise for Israel is intended to support the exilic claim over the Judaean position.'[23] Carroll's rejection of a real preaching of repentance by Jeremiah, therefore, is bound up with his wider view of the nature and composition of the book. His line of argument here, however, involves serious improbabilities. The identification of 'Judah' with the post-exilic Palestinian community, as distinct from the returning exiles, lacks any analogy. In Carroll's treatment of chapter 3, in fact, 'Israel' really means Judah, and 'Judah' really means a hypothetical group within the post-exilic community. In his view the discourse of chapters 2 – 3 is, therefore, unyieldingly enigmatic. It is hard to avoid the conclusion that his understanding of the book as a whole has in this case at least militated against good exegesis.

It remains to consider the second answer offered above, that Jeremiah did in fact preach repentance to Judah at some point in his ministry prior to the exile. This is the position which is most likely to be right. It was adopted, as we saw, by McKane, on the basis of his interpretation of verses 12f. His view depended, however, on the simple identification of 'Israel' as Judah. This we have seen, however, to be unconvincing. Rather, the names 'Israel' and 'Judah' are so used throughout chapter 2 as to place the latter's experience in the context of the whole history of Israel, with particular reminiscences of the north. McKane's view, furthermore, depends on the general belief that the chapter consists of parts which lack coherence with each other, and which derive from diverse settings. This observation illustrates that it cannot be supposed that Jeremiah preached repentance to Judah without careful consideration. Rather, it involves an understanding of the composition of the text. It is time, therefore, to draw some conclusions on the matter from our discussion so far.

The main plank in the platform of both McKane and Carroll in their argument for the composite nature of the chapter was that the author of verses 6–11 had misunderstood and misapplied the use of 'Israel' in 3:1–5. Our own account of 2:4 – 3:5, however, presents a challenge to their view. It is not the case that 'Israel' simply refers to Judah. Rather, the use of the name is complex, and allows the history of the northern kingdom to stand as a warning or threat over Judah. This aspect of the use of the term in 2:4 – 3:5 means that the thought in verses 6–11 may be seen as a legitimate development of 3:1–5. Verses 12f. are also consistent with the train of thought in the chapter up to this point. The rhetorical character of the verses does not require that they should have been spoken directly to the former northern kingdom. Rather, they proclaim before Judah, in a stylized way, what YHWH still says to a people whose faithlessness eventually led to exile.

From repentance to redemption

Verses 12f., indeed, cannot be understood apart from what follows them. Verses 14–18 are clearly linked to them by their opening phrase: 'Return, O faithless children', a variation of verse 12. As we have already seen, a new note is now sounded, namely YHWH's redemption of his people beyond exile. The stylized address to the north (12f.) therefore becomes a way of conceptualizing before Judah the idea that for her too there lies a way back to God beyond an exile which she in turn must endure.

With verses 12–18, therefore, we have a major theological development in the thought of the chapter. Yet it too belongs to the discussion to which verses 1–5 give rise. The issue in verse 1 was, on the surface, whether Israel would return to YHWH. This was taken up in verses 7 and 10, yet there is a profounder issue in verses 1–5, suggested both by the law of Deuteronomy 24:1–4 which underlies them, and by verse 5 itself, namely, whether YHWH will return to Israel. This question begins to be answered in verse 12, and gains a fuller development in verses 14–18.

We begin to see how much the text before us is the result of theological reflection. Verses 12–18, in fact, represent its heart. The section 3:19 – 4:4 takes up the basic themes in a new way. Verses 19–20 resume the central problem of verses 1–5, the tendency of Israel to turn away from YHWH, taking up the term 'faithless' from verses 12 and 14. Verses 22b–24 then depict a repentance of Israel, in specific response to verse 22a. Yet the matter has hardly reached a satisfactory issue with this confession. As we have noticed above, the terms in which the appeal of verse 22a is couched are ominous in their suggestion that Judah cannot repent in truth. Furthermore, the continuation from 3:22b–24, namely 4:1–4, immediately puts Israel's true repentance back into question. The appeal to Judah to 'Circumcise yourselves to the LORD' (4) seems to convey the passion of an actual exhortation of the prophet. Yet the final note is threatening, and an all too appropriate preparation for the next cycle of sayings, in which the inevitability of the coming judgment is dominant (4:5 – 6:30). Even if chapter 3, therefore, has shown the way to *Jeremiah*'s solution of the problem of Judah's persistent rebelliousness, the focus now comes firmly back to imminent judgment on her sin.

Conclusions

We began with the question whether there was evidence in *Jeremiah* 3 for a preaching of repentance by Jeremiah which held out real hope of a response sufficient to avert the judgment of YHWH. Our study has shown how difficult it is to answer the question with confidence. It is likely, indeed, that a passage such as 4:1–4, viewed as an originally separate oracle, furnishes good evidence of repentance preaching which hoped for a favourable response. Because of the shape of its context, however, that evidence is only of a rather indirect nature. We do not, in other words, have mere transcripts of Jeremiah's oracles. Rather, they are mediated to us by a process of reflection which incorporates developments on a theme. It does not follow from this observation, in my view, that the coherence of this reflection must be attributed to some nameless 'redaction'. Holladay's belief that Jeremiah himself could have masterminded the collection of his own sayings, and thus provided a testimony to his own developing thought, is quite as good an option.

In any case, the reflection on the theme of repentance knows of Judah's ultimate and decisive failure to repent (*e.g.* 3:10). This failure poses the question how YHWH can henceforth deal with his people. One answer is supplied by the pictures of judgment in 4:5 – 6:30. Another is contained in 3:15–18, which appears to look beyond the exile ('in those days') to an idealized reunification of Judah and Israel. Furthermore, 3:22a resolves the meditation on the theme of Judah's 'returning' by making YHWH the author of it, so that he himself creates a new relationship in terms which anticipate those of the 'new covenant' (*cf.* 23:4; 31:31, 33). In the final text, therefore, the repentance, or returning, enjoined upon Judah has the connotation of restoration to the land.

The chapter as a whole, then, answers the double question which was posed in 3:1–5, namely (a) 'would you [Israel/Judah] return to me?' (1) – YHWH's question expecting, and getting, the answer no; and (b) 'will he [YHWH] be angry for ever?' (5) – Israel's question expecting, and ultimately also getting, the answer no. Yet the tension between these two answers is such that this 'no' cannot follow without huge convulsions, both in Judah's life and in her theologizing. The remainder of the book of Jeremiah is the story of those convulsions.

It remains only to comment on the use of the 'returning' motif here in comparison with its use in DtH. The two usages are in fact quite distinct. Although 'returning' is a strong theme in DtH, it does not equate with restoration to the land. The clearest example of this is in Solomon's prayer at 1 Kings 8:46–53, which directly addresses the eventuality of exile. In that place, the only passage in Kings which explicitly looks beyond the exile, 'returning' means a turning back to YHWH which conspicuously falls short of restoration to the land. (1 Ki. 8:34 does not have in view a return to the land following exile. It addresses rather the case of defeat in battle, which may indeed result in some deportations, but which does not prevent a corporate act of penitence *in* the temple; contrast verse 48: *'toward their land – and the house'*.) In this respect Kings stops short of the hope expressed in Deuteronomy 30:3. *Jeremiah* stands much closer to that hope. In relation to Deuteronomy 30:3, therefore, Kings and *Jeremiah* represent distinct developments.[24] The separate paths taken by Kings and *Jeremiah* on 'returning' illustrate how unsatisfactory it is to think of *Jeremiah* as 'Deuteronomistic'.

CHAPTER TWO

Deferral of hope (1 – 24)

In the previous chapter, we have seen an example of the treatment of the idea of hope for Judah. There was evidence in *Jeremiah* 3 that hope had once been held out for averting the exile altogether. In the present form of the book, however, such hope had given way to the knowledge that the exile would come, and that the way forward for Judah with YHWH would be on the basis of a new kind of relationship. Similar observations, indeed, can be made as we look beyond chapter 3. The Temple sermon, for example (7:1–15), furnishes evidence of a real preaching for repentance by Jeremiah, because of its implication that if the people cease from their wicked ways they will even yet be permitted to dwell in the land (5–7). Further evidence of a different sort occurs, paradoxically, in the thrice-issued command of Jeremiah not to pray for the people (implying that he might otherwise have done so, in the hope that they would repent), 7:16; 11:14; 15:1. Finally, 17:19–27 might be placed in this category, though that passage raises problems of its own.[1]

As in the case of the repentance preaching which we examined in *Jeremiah* 3, however, the contexts of passages of this sort show again that the proffered hope of averting the exile was not the prophet's final word. The point is abundantly clear, for example, in the prohibitions of intercessory prayer (one of which immediately follows the Temple sermon, at 7:16). Our interest in the present chapter is to develop the point thus introduced, namely to examine the nature of the treatment of hope for Judah in the first 24 chapters of the book. In this task it is impossible to separate any statement from the context it has been given. The thesis we wish to present is that these chapters testify first to a closing down of hope for a repentance which might avert the disaster of exile, then to the offer of a new kind of hope, which, however, is deferred until the judgment has been experienced. There is in addition a new element, not yet mentioned, namely the modelling of hope for the survival of judgment in the person of Jeremiah. (We shall consider this separately in the following chapter.) It is worth reiterating that our quest is not for the historical development of Jeremiah's preaching, but for an interpretation of the event of exile now enshrined in the book that contains his prophecies. This being so, we are interested in all the material, without raising at this point in our study, the issue of 'authenticity'.

We have seen that our chapters afford evidence of a preaching of repentance and hope. Taken as a whole, however, the first half of the book of *Jeremiah* makes an impact that is far more ominous than hopeful. (The prophet of doom does not have his reputation for nothing.) We have seen this to be so in 3:1 – 4:4. Other features of the early chapters join with that passage to depict Judah as evil to the point of irredeemability.

The theme of falsehood (*šeqer*) is one of the special characteristics of Judah's apostasy as presented in *Jeremiah*, developed particularly in 8:22 – 9:8.[2] Because of the depth of the people's depravity, there is a sense of despair in some of the words of YHWH spoken by the prophet. In 6:29 we find:

> 'in vain the refining (*ṣrp*) goes on,
>   for the wicked are not removed.'

And the idea of refining recurs in 9:7, in the context of the passage referred to concerning Judah's falsehood, not because there is good hope of success by such refining, but out of a kind of necessity born of YHWH's attachment to his people: 'for what else can I do, because of my people?' Judah's temerity goes so far as to defy YHWH. Her disobedience is deeper than mere moral weakness or turpitude. It is an ideological rejection of the word of God. The people say of YHWH:

> 'He will do nothing;
> no evil will come upon us'

and

> 'The prophets will become wind;
> the word is not in them.' (5:12–13)

Word-rejection is important in the whole thematic development of the book.[3] There is a certain double-edged quality to Jeremiah's polemic against the prophets on the one hand, and against the people on the other for not listening to 'the prophets'. (This will give rise in due course to the treatment of the question: who is a prophet? – as in chapter 28.) The faithlessness of the prophets, however, clearly does not exonerate the people from the charge of treating the word with contempt (cf. 7:25–26).

The presumption of Judah is taken up again in the Temple sermon, with the introduction of the argument about Shiloh. Do the people think that they are secure because of the mere possession of the Temple, the place which YHWH chose for his name? Was not Shiloh the place where YHWH's name dwelt at first? Yet, as Jeremiah's hearers knew well, there was no surviving sign of Shiloh, which had been destroyed, presumably, in some Philistine aggression (7:12–15).[4]

A people that cannot repent; a people given over to falsehood; a people that will not accept YHWH's word, yet places unthinking trust in his Temple: already in this picture there is material which belongs naturally within an explanation of inevitable punishment. The use of the term gôy (nation) for Judah belongs within the pattern. Jeremiah, of course, is called to be a prophet to the nations (gôyim, 1:5), and the term occurs frequently throughout the book of *Jeremiah*.

Often there is a contrast between Israel/Judah, the *'am* (people) of YHWH, and the other *gôyim*, familiar in other Old Testament literature. (12:16–17 expressly place the *gôyim* in contrast to 'my people', *'ammî*; other passages where the *gôyim* exclude Judah are 10:25; 22:8.) Furthermore, 4:2 takes up the terms of Genesis 22:18, with its idea of the nations blessing themselves in Israel.[5] In the framework of the whole book, Jeremiah's mission to the nations is finally fulfilled when he delivers the oracles of chapters 46 – 51, and especially those against Babylon.[6]

Predominantly, however, the *gôy* motif is used in the book to imply that Judah is a *gôy* like any other. The point is made forcefully in a recurring phrase:

> 'Shall I not punish them for these things? says the LORD;
> and shall I not avenge myself
> on a nation (*gôy*) such as this?' (5:9, 29; 9:9; *cf.* 7:28)

This refrain is the most striking case of Judah being classed with the nations in a way that puts a new light on Jeremiah's call to be a prophet to the nations. In addition, however, there are instances where the formal contrast between Israel/Judah and the nations is maintained, but where the effect is to diminish the difference, or even to put the covenant people in a worse light than their neighbours. One such is 2:11:

> 'Has a nation (*gôy*) changed its gods,
> even though they are no gods?
> But my people (*'ammî*) have changed their glory
> for that which does not profit.'

Another is 9:24–25, which announces YHWH's intention to punish nations that are 'circumcised but yet uncircumcised'. Not only does the ensuing list include Judah, but the train of thought continues with an argument that once again puts 'Israel' in an even worse light: 'for all these nations are uncircumcised, and all the house of Israel is uncircumcised in heart' (26).

Finally in this connection, it is important to note a minor theme in the book relating to the nations, namely hints of their salvation. This admittedly lacks the proportions in *Jeremiah* which it assumes in other prophetic literature, especially Isaiah. It occurs first, however, at 3:17, in terms somewhat reminiscent of Isaiah 2:2f. (*cf.* Mi. 4:1f.), and recurs at 12:14–17, where language belonging to the special relationship between YHWH and Israel ('land', 'heritage') is applied to the nations. In both these places (as in the Isaiah passage) the salvation of the nations seems to be mediated somehow by Israel. A further case in point is 16:19, where the idea of Israel's mediation is less strong. And in 46:26; 48:47 and 49:6, 39 restoration following exile will be promised to Egypt, Moab, Ammon and Elam respectively, in terms which echo those in which a similar promise is held out to Israel and Judah in the 'Book of Consolation'.[7] Also in those parts of the book which speak of salvation, therefore, there is an element which diminishes the special status of Israel.

In this first half of *Jeremiah* however, the emphasis falls still on imminent judgment. And in this connection, the analogy between Israel/Judah and the nations gains deliberate further development in the first visit of Jeremiah to the potter. Having seen the pot spoiled and remade in the hands of the potter, Jeremiah addresses a word to the 'house of Israel' (18:6), which is framed so as to have reference to any 'nation or kingdom' (7–9). The same suppression of all significant difference between Judah and other nations is pursued in those passages which describe Nebuchadrezzar's mission from YHWH (25:9, 11, 18; 27:7–8, 11; 28:11, 14).

There is thus a theme in the book, strongly present in both prose and poetry, which tends to play down the covenant status of Judah. One result is to put Jeremiah's mission to the nations in a new light. That mission is not merely to be understood as directed to the nations other than Judah, though that is part of it; it has a side which is, initially at least, darker for Judah, namely that the prophet comes to her on

47

the basis of a call to 'the nations', as much as on that of Judah's covenant status. That status is rendered ambivalent by the nations theme in the book, which thus contributes to the picture of a Judah whose privileges with YHWH are at an end.

The nations theme also forges a link between the books of *Jeremiah* and Kings. In the latter it surfaces at 2 Kings 17, in which exiled Israel is replaced in the northern territory by other nations brought in by Assyria. That passage contains an account (17:24–28) of how the king of Assyria brought a priest of YHWH to teach the nations his law (*tôrâ*). The result is no better than syncretistic worship on their part (33–41). The purpose of the account seems to be to show how Israel and Judah had been no better than the nations. The effect of the nations theme in 2 Kings 17, as in *Jeremiah*, therefore, is to diminish the status of the covenant people. Kings, however, does not take the step, which we have noticed in *Jeremiah*, of holding out the hope of salvation to the nations. On the contrary, the abortive teaching of the law of YHWH to the nations in 2 Kings 17 even parodies the eschatological vision in Isaiah 2:2–4, in which the nations join Israel in seeking it.

Two more features strike at the continuing validity of the covenant in Jeremiah's preaching. The first is the imagery of devastation in 4:23–27, which goes beyond picturing Judah laid waste and evokes a whole created order destroyed by the breach in relations between Judah and her God. The use of *'ereṣ* in these verses is ambiguous as between the land of Israel and the whole earth; and there are other allusions to the creation story of Genesis 1, and indeed the dependent account of the covenant with the whole earth in Genesis 9 (heavens, man [*hā'āḏām*], birds of the air). Not only is the covenant with Israel at stake, but the covenant with all mankind.

Finally, there is a telling *non sequitur* related to the idea of Israel's election in 10:16–17. The passage 10:1–16 is an extended hymn to YHWH in his incomparability. In its content, it resembles parts of Isaiah 40 – 55, and for this reason may be thought to be directed in particular against Babylonian deities, and to be datable to the exilic or post-exilic period. In fact it has been variously assessed as to unity of authorship. Overholt and Holladay, for example, defend Jeremianic authorship,[8] while others date it later, and see it as composite in origin. Carroll finds the ethos of the poem 'so very different from that of the rest of the book that it is difficult to see how Jeremiah could have uttered it'.[9] His reasoning focuses on the sympathetic tone in which Israel is addressed, and the absence of any criticism of her idolatry or unjust practices.

Yet Carroll's inability to attribute the poem to Jeremiah derives in part from his own understanding of the nature of the Jeremianic tradition. If the tradition is approached, however, with a higher estimate of the function of juxtapositions in conveying meaning, different results are suggested. The climax of the hymn (16) strikes first the theme of creation ('he is the one who formed all things'), then of election ('Israel is the tribe of his inheritance'). In itself, this note would indeed sit uncomfortably with Jeremiah's challenges elsewhere to over-casual reliance on the election traditions (as in 7:1–15), though it is in fact not incompatible with his call to be a prophet to the nations and his final words of judgment against Babylon. In the immediate context, however, the juxtaposition with what follows, in verses 17–18, is dramatic:

> Gather up your bundle from the ground,
>   O you who dwell under siege!
> For thus says the LORD:
> 'Behold, I am slinging out the inhabitants of the land
>   at this time,
> and I will bring distress on them,
>   that they may feel it.'

The hymn on the incomparability of YHWH thus functions on different levels. In itself, it anticipates the final judgment of YHWH against Babylon, the oppressor of his people, and may have been uttered originally in some context, perhaps late in Jeremiah's ministry, in which that was its

49

primary aim. In its present literary setting, however, it produces, together with what follows, a telling *non sequitur*, which expresses powerfully the folly of wrong reliance on the election tradition, even though that tradition in itself is well grounded. The progression of thought from verses 1–16 to verses 17–18 well illustrates the manner in which the Jeremiah tradition reflects theologically. *Non sequitur* is used here to proclaim judgment. Later in the book it will be used with equal effectiveness to announce salvation.[10] For the moment, however, the feature belongs to the drift of Jeremiah's demonstration that Judah has no hope of escaping judgment.

The foregoing shows that, in a general way, the first half of the book of *Jeremiah* presents the prophet's preaching to the reader in such a way as to suggest that there is little prospect of averting the predicted punishment. The incapacity of Judah to repent, however, and the consequent inevitability of punishment, are made even more explicit by certain features which we have not yet mentioned. These are features which clearly go further than conventional prophetic adumbrations of judgment.

The prohibition of intercession

The first such feature is YHWH's repeated prohibition of intercession by Jeremiah (7:16; 11:14; 15:1). The background to such prohibitions is often considered to be a recognized intercessory role on the part of the prophet,[11] though not always.[12] The evidence for it depends, like so much else, on how extensive one considers the influence of the Deuteronomists. Amos 7:1–6, however, is certainly a precedent for such a role. And Genesis 18:23–33; 20:7; Exodus 32:11–14 and 1 Samuel 7:5–11; 12:19–23 testify to the existence of the concept even if the dating of the passages is a matter of debate.[13]

More important is the mere fact that in Jeremiah the prophet is actually associated with the intercessory role. In

15:1 Moses and Samuel are invoked precisely to appeal to their potency as intercessors. This appeal creates all the background necessary for the prohibition, repeated three times, to stand out as a feature of the portrayal of Jeremiah's ministry in this part of the book.[14] In each of the three cases YHWH addresses himself directly to the prophet, not to the people, and Jeremiah never overtly turns the command of YHWH to account in his exhortation to the people. The clear implication, therefore, is that YHWH's mind is now fixed on a course of action from which it cannot be turned. There is a note of resolution in his utterances which shows how appropriate is his deafness to pleas for Judah, in response to Judah's deafness to his many past appeals to her to repent (with 7:16 *cf.* 7:13). It seems that there is more here than simple prophetic hyperbole.

An ancillary point may be made in connection with the prohibition in chapter 15. In 15:4 YHWH says:

> 'And I will make them a horror to all the kingdoms of the earth because of what Manasseh the son of Hezekiah, king of Judah, did in Jerusalem.'

The allusion to Manasseh is remarkable in a book which gives so much more prominence to the blameworthiness of Josiah's successors. This, indeed, is the only allusion to Manasseh in the book. The manner of the reference, furthermore, recalls the appeal to the sins of the same king in 2 Kings 23:26 as the decisive reason for the punishment of Judah even in spite of the reforms of Josiah. It is hard to think that there is not some allusion to the Kings passage at this point in the prophecy. If so, it is an appeal to another passage which speaks of YHWH's mind set on punishment despite factors which might have predisposed him otherwise (in the case of Kings, Josiah's reform; in *Jeremiah*, the prophet's prayer). The introduction of Manasseh at this particular point, therefore, strengthens the implication in the prohibition to intercede that there is now no mercy for Judah this side of judgment.

Two visits to the potter

A second example of the closing down of hope in the structuring of the first half of the book is the treatment of the potter theme in 18:1–12 and chapter 19. It is remarkable, at first glance, that Jeremiah should receive two commands to visit the potter. There have, predictably, been explanations of the phenomenon in terms of disparate settings for the parts of the two passages in question. *Jeremiah* 18:1–12 especially has been thought to be a composition of diverse parts. Thiel's analysis of the passage into three parts (1–6, 7–10, 11f.) has been broadly accepted by both Carroll and McKane.[15] It is interesting, however, that the latter two differ diametrically on the meaning of verses 1–6. Carroll regards the passage as a 'positive, optimistic metaphor of hope for the future',[16] while McKane declares that it 'proclaims unconditional doom for Judah'![17] The contrast is a telling illustration of the deficiencies of the premiss shared by both, namely that the text combines variations on a theme, in such a way as to result in a more or less incoherent discourse. Both treatments are also ambivalent about the Deuteronomistic character of verses 7–10. Carroll sees the extension of the principle of 'turning', typical of the Deuteronomist, to embrace the nations, as going beyond the Deuteronomist, and 'an even later development within the Jeremiah tradition'.[18] McKane says that verses 7–11 '*embody* Deuteronomic theology' (my italics), and that they represent 'a later theorizing and a drawing out of the crucial function of repentance in the Deuteronomic scheme'.[19]

In fact, there are good reasons to see 18:1–12 as both coherent and distinctively 'Jeremianic'. Carroll's and McKane's basic difference of opinion as to the meaning of verses 1–6 suggests that the passage in itself is ambiguous or incomplete, and requires some continuation. Verse 11, sometimes thought to be a more appropriate continuation from verses 1–6 than verses 7–10,[20] is insufficient in itself, because it does not take up the idea of reshaping. Verses 7–10, therefore, are a necessary interpretation of verses 1–6 (*pace* McKane), and in line with a feature of the *Jeremiah* tradition which we have observed, namely the setting of YHWH's treatment of Judah in the context of his attitude to the nations.

Our interest in the purpose of the discourse, however, falls on the relationship between the two incidents. (At this point we differ sharply once again from most 'Deuteronomistic' interpretations.) In the first (18:1–12) the prophet simply observes the craftsman making, breaking, then remaking a pot, and draws an analogy with Israel in the hands of God (18:4–6). The passage thus pictures the possibility of salvation for Judah. YHWH can act either in judgment or affirmation. All depends on Judah's repentance. The first potter incident is thus a call to repent. The tenor of the remainder of the chapter, however, lays emphasis upon the stubbornness of Judah and the imminence of judgment. The picture of possible salvation gives way to the bleaker prospects of a nation that insists on its own doom.

That trend continues, more interestingly, in the resumption of the potter theme in chapter 19. Now Jeremiah is commanded to *buy* an earthen flask (1), and to proceed to break it in full view of elders and people (10). The flask is to be broken 'so that it can never be mended' (11). The second potter incident thus completes the first. Whereas the first opens up the possibility of repentance and salvation, the second closes it down. The deliberate arrangement of these passages in relation to each other shows that there is more here than conventional prophetic judgment symbolism. Rather, there is a story which opens a particular avenue on to the future, only to show in the end that the future does not lie that way. The twofold potter incident is part of the unfolding, in the first part of the book, of the ineluctability of exile.

Deferral of hope in passages concerning the future

Paradoxically, a further category of passages which speak of the inevitability of punishment is constituted by those which also show that there will be a future beyond the disaster. We have already observed one of these in chapter 3, where, in verses 14–18, the command to 'return!' is evidently a command to return from exile to reoccupy the land, and the phrases 'in those days' (16, 18) show that the event in question is remote from the period in which Jeremiah is actually conducting his ministry.

A similar glimpse into the future is afforded by 16:14–15. Chapter 16 is interesting as a whole because it contains words to Jeremiah which bear a certain similarity to the prohibition to pray, discussed above. Here, the prophet is prohibited from either marrying, entering the house of mourning, or feasting. The first (2–4) is a parable of the fact that Judah has no future of the sort which the giving and taking in marriage normally implies. The second (5–7) illustrates a future so bleak that there will not be mourning even for those who die. And the last (8–9) simply foreshadows the passing of all gladness.

In themselves these would count as conventional prophetic symbolism. They become more definitive than that for two reasons. First, the glimpse into the future, in verses 14–16, shows that in fact the only way through the sufferings pronounced by the prophet is by way of exile. Second, these prohibitions upon Jeremiah have their counterpart in symbolic acts in the latter part of the book which are designed to reopen hope (such as Jeremiah's acquisition of a field; see below, chapter 4). The force of *Jeremiah* 16 as a whole is to make clear that the way of future hope is through the suffering of exile.

Transition and kingship: chapters 21 – 24

The transition from imminent punishment to a doctrine of hope that lies beyond it is contained, however, not only in glimpses of this sort. Rather, it receives sustained treatment in chapters 21 – 24. This section opens and closes with words to and about King Zedekiah. The chronology of the book is remarkable enough in itself at this point. Zedekiah is the last king of the Davidic line, the one who will preside in the end over the failure of Judah to avert the Babylonian threat. His introduction at this stage of the prophecy focuses attention on its full chronological span, and indeed on its outcome. Chapter 21 itself falls into the category of those passages which are unequivocal about Judah's immediate doom.

The chapter opens with an embassy to Jeremiah from Zedekiah via Pashhur the son of Malchiah (not the Pashhur who behaved violently to Jeremiah in 20:2, though there are thematic links between the two passages: *cf.* Carroll).[21] Since it follows the second potter incident, with its closing down of hope, and the prophet's own cry of despair in 20:14–18 (see further below), it is difficult for the reader, as perhaps it was for Zedekiah, to attach much confidence to his words 'perhaps the LORD will deal with us according to all his wonderful deeds, and will make him [Nebuchadrezzar] withdraw from us' (2). Zedekiah's appeal to the theme of holy war, in these words, rebounds ironically in Jeremiah's reply that, in the coming engagement, YHWH will be fighting on the other side (5)!

What decisively sets this exchange apart from a conventional prophetic warning that intends to produce repentance, however, is the declaration in verses 8–10. In these verses there is a twist on the Deuteronomic appeal to choose between the ways of life and death (Dt. 30:19), which consists in a choice of obedience to YHWH, resulting in continued enjoyment of the land. In fact, the gap between our passage and the one alluded to in Deuteronomy is not very great, because the wider context of the latter also knows that there must be an exile before there can be true enjoyment of the covenant blessings (see 30:1–6). Nevertheless, *Jeremiah* uses the phrase in question in a particular and surprising way. Its appeal is not simply to righteous living but to acceptance of the Babylonian yoke (9b).

From this point the thought arcs forward to the vision in chapter 24 which again features Zedekiah, and reiterates the message about subjugation to Babylon. The intervening material concerns the kings of Judah more generally. It contains material which is not chronologically marked, such as 21:12–14, which is, in itself, a conventional word of judgment against an oppressor. The context in which words of this sort now stand, however, is one which takes further the thought developed in 21:1–10.

Chapter 22 contains the most sustained accusation of kings in the book, together with YHWH's verdict on them. Its thrust is that there is no hope for the future in the Davidic line. In pursuing the point, it does so in a quite different way from the books of Kings. There, the ultimate inadequacy of the historical Davidic dynasty was expressed in heavily ironic terms, with the slide into exile following hard on the heels of an account of the faithfulness of Josiah. The method adopted there required a celebration of the reign of Josiah, which would stand in stark contrast with the narrative of the ensuing events.[22] *Jeremiah* 22, in contrast, passes lightly over the success of Josiah, using it only to sharpen the criticism of his successors (15–16). The difference between *Jeremiah* 22 and 2 Kings 22 and 23, indeed, typifies the difference between the two corpora. Kings concentrates on the dynasty up to Josiah, focuses its explanation of the exile on the sequence Manasseh – Josiah, and passes quickly over Josiah's successors. These, though themselves wicked, are not in the centre of the explanation of exile according to the method of Kings. *Jeremiah* on the other hand, glances back only briefly at the dynasty up to and including Josiah, and directs its fire chiefly at Josiah's successors, not only in this chapter, but in all the important confrontations with kings in the book.

The difference between the books consists, so far, not in separate evaluations of the individual kings, but in style and approach. *Jeremiah*'s concentration on the end of the dynasty, however, has two consequences which set the book apart from Kings. First, it allows a more categorical pronouncement of the dynasty's failure. The declaration that Jehoiachin

(=Coniah) will have no offspring to sit on the throne of David (22:30) makes it impossible to interpret the release of the same king, recorded in *Jeremiah* 52:31–34 just as in 2 Kings 25:27–30, as an expression of hope for the coming restoration of the monarchy.[23] Jeremiah's recorded altercations with Jehoiakim (via Baruch and the princes in chapter 36) and Zedekiah (chapters 34, 37 and 38) are a kind of mopping-up operation in which it becomes plain that the dynasty is breathing its sorry last. We shall return to these in due course, in the context of an interpretation of the later parts of the book (see below, chapters 4 – 5). Because it is germane to the immediate point, however, namely the respective evaluations of the historical dynasty in *Jeremiah* and Kings, it is in place here to pinpoint the similarities and differences between Jehoiakim's reaction to Jeremiah's words and the reaction of Josiah to the discovery of the 'book of the law' in 2 Kings 22.

Jehoiakim and Josiah

It has been widely observed that the two accounts in question have close parallels.[24] As Josiah is confronted by a discovery, so too there is an air of discovery in the bringing of Jeremiah's words to the king. When Gemariah the son of Shaphan hears a public reading of the prophet's words and brings news of it to the 'princes' (11–12), they react in alarm, as if all this was quite fresh to them (16–19). Their response, indeed, is reminiscent of Josiah's, and in this context, makes a striking contrast with that of Jehoiakim. A further obvious similarity between the two events is in the matter of a book-reading itself: the king is not confronted by the prophet in the flesh, but by a formalized account of his words.

The drawing of these similarities apparently has the purpose of sharpening the contrast between the two kings. Jehoiakim's studied impiety could not be in greater contrast to Josiah's pious response. The one king attempts to let the words have their full effect; the other does what he can to destroy their power.[25] Paradoxically, however, the two accounts ultimately have the same effect. Comparisons of the two passages have usually been over-simple because of the general failure to recognize the real function of the account of Josiah's reform.[26] Those who take the portrayal of Josiah in Kings to be a model of the Davidic king and a basis for future hope see the picture of Jehoiakim as an ironic comment on the failure of the dynasty to sustain the hopes which Josiah aroused. In our view, however, Kings has its own irony. The recognition of this, furthermore, has the effect that the two passages are at heart similar in their intention. The real difference between them, in their evaluations of the historical dynasty, is one of method and approach. There is a consistency, therefore, in *Jeremiah*'s manner of allusion to Josiah, whether explicitly as in chapter 22, or implicitly as in chapter 36. His righteousness is not in doubt. But *Jeremiah* may be seen as accepting the premiss of Kings that righteousness could not issue in salvation for Judah. It then proceeds to handle that theological datum in its own way.

The second consequence of the special handling of the historical dynasty in *Jeremiah* with its concentration on its final kings, is the manner in which, having buried it, it resuscitates it. This occurs initially in the great *non sequitur* of 23:5–6, where YHWH declares that he will 'raise up for David a righteous Branch'. As *Jeremiah* is more categorical than Kings about the end of the historical dynasty, so it is more categorical about an act of YHWH that will transcend its demise. Chapters 22 and 23, therefore, form a suitable prelude to the vision in chapter 24 in which the future of Judah is shown to lie along a path which expressly excludes King Zedekiah. They play their part in a story which tells of a failure of the nation that brings irrevocable punishment in its train, but which opens on to a new kind of salvation beyond. It is in this transcendence of the historical dynasty, rather than in its view of Josiah, that *Jeremiah* decisively embraces a different solution to the problem of kingship from Kings.

With chapter 24 comes a new statement of the impossibility of averting the coming catastrophe in the time of

Zedekiah, and a repetition of the idea (from 21:8–10) that the future of Judahites now depends on their attitude to YHWH's appointed instrument of punishment, Babylon. The incident recorded here is a vision given and explained to Jeremiah. The 'good figs' of the vision are those who have already been sent away to Babylon. Through these, YHWH's purposes for his people will continue; their destiny is restoration to the land and a new heart to know him.

The function of the vision is revelation, not exhortation, and in a way *Jeremiah* has reached its first climax by this point. Its prominence in the structure of the book is heightened, incidentally, by the observation that the vision occurs chronologically prior to the exchange with Zedekiah in 21:1–10 (*i.e.* in the context of Nebuchadrezzar's earlier attentions to Judah rather than his final depredations in 587–586 BC). The vision serves, indeed, as a kind of interpretation of the whole prophecy. As a retrospect on chapters 1 – 23 it confirms what we have argued is the force of those chapters taken together, namely to show that there is no immediate hope for Judah. Because of the intervening argument since chapter 21, the undercurrent is present that, in particular, there is no hope of immediate salvation through the historical dynasty. Rather, YHWH has other plans, which lie beyond exile, and envisage a king who is radically different from any yet known. There is, therefore, a very positive message to *Jeremiah* 24 (expressed particularly in verse 7), and indeed the chapter makes clear links with parts of the second half of the book (*e.g.* 29:12–14; 31:31–34), to which we shall return. For the moment, it is important to see it as a crucial point in the composition of the whole book, marking a transition from the theology of inevitable doom to the theology of a new kind of future with YHWH such as Judah has not yet dreamed of.[27]

Conclusions

In the present chapter we have seen that, as in 3:1 – 4:4, the remainder of the first half of *Jeremiah* (to chapter 24) testifies to an understanding of YHWH's purposes for Judah which knows that the only hope of a future covenantal relationship lies beyond an exile. As was the case with 3:1 – 4:4, so it is of the whole redaction of 1 – 24, that its understanding of Judah's future with YHWH is distinct from that of Kings, which does not look beyond the exile. This was so even though at certain points *Jeremiah* has important affinities with Kings, *e.g.* in the underlying attitudes of both corpora to the historic Davidic dynasty. A further difference between the two related to the nations. Although both *Jeremiah* and 2 Kings 17 used the nations theme in such a way as to diminish the covenant status of Israel, *Jeremiah* went beyond this by including the nations, albeit by way of a minor theme, in the vision of YHWH's new work of salvation beyond the exile. On other grounds too, we saw that the use of the term 'Deuteronomistic' of the redaction of *Jeremiah* was hard to sustain with consistency. It was based furthermore on a premiss of the incoherence of the redaction, which equally could not be sustained in detail. Our own approach, in contrast, pictures a redaction which has a certain consistent tendency, and which we are justified in calling Jeremianic, not Deuteronomistic.

CHAPTER THREE

Hope and the figure of Jeremiah (Jeremiah's Confessions)

Having attempted to understand the main theological tendency of *Jeremiah* 1 – 24, it is important to consider a special question in the interpretation of this part of the book, namely the function of the prophet himself. It needs no demonstration that the figure of Jeremiah plays a more prominent role in the prophecy that bears his name than any other prophet does in his. This would be true even apart from the third-person accounts which become frequent in the latter half of the book. His pronouncements of judgment upon the people, in what usually passes for his early ministry, are marked by expressions of personal distress. *Jeremiah* 4:19 and 10:19 illustrate well how these two features mesh; Jeremiah's distress is of a piece with the message. He feels already the pain that will come upon the people, in a way that proves his identification with them.

Our present question is to what extent the portrayal of Jeremiah coheres with and serves the message of the book. It belongs in fact to a central theological struggle in the book, namely the question: what is a true prophet, and which of those 'prophets', who were prominent in the life of the people in the days before exile, truly had the authority to speak for YHWH? Chapter 23 brings together the motif of YHWH's future plans (20) and the capacity of the prophets to know and speak them (21–22). The picture of prophets trading lies (25–32) invites the question, how can the people know when they hear God's word? The salvation-prophets, after all, are saying things which are in keeping with what Israel has been taught to believe about her God.[1] Jeremiah, on the other hand, has a message which requires the people to believe that there is no immediate hope, and that the present judgment will bear fruit in a greater salvation in the future. The message requires a vindication of the man.

The problem gives rise to the well-known confrontation between Jeremiah and the salvation-prophets, especially Hananiah (chapter 28).[2] Jeremiah's triumph over Hananiah, however, is not his final word. For his message is bound up with his own suffering, which has been part of his announcement of the suffering which the people too must endure. His identification with them in this way forces an interpretation of his experience, which cannot be detached from his message.

The prophet's identification with the people, however, is inseparable from his identification with the will of YHWH, which condemns the people's sin. If the prophet feels keenly the horror of the 'alarm of war' (4:19), he feels equally keenly the stupidity and evil of the people (4:22). Between these two identifications lies a contradiction which develops within the prophet's personality, until the great cry of self-loathing in 20:14–18. The tension is unfolded in the sections known to scholarship as Jeremiah's Confessions. In these utterances (*viz.* 11:18–23; 12:1–6; 15:10–14, 15–21; 17:14–18; 18:18–23; 20:7–13, 14–18)[3] the prophet's pain deriving from his ministry turns to sometimes bitter protest at his calling. Their address to YHWH, together with their unrestrained tone, characterizes them as a separate group.

The Confessions have a history of interpretation all of their own, reflecting both their uniqueness and difficulty, on the one hand, and the path of scholarly discussion of prophecy in general, on the other. Two parallel questions are raised by them: first, as to their setting in the life of Jeremiah, and secondly, as to their setting in the life of the nation, if any. A special part of the latter concerns their present setting in the book of Jeremiah.

In the heyday of literary criticism, with its undertone of liberal piety, the emphasis fell squarely on the place of the Confessions in the life of the prophet. They became the parade example of that individual religious sensitivity which was said to mark the development of Old Testament religion away from the mechanism and materialism of the cult. Skinner's exposition of Jeremiah along these lines fitted well with Duhm's confinement of what was 'authentically' prophetic to the lyrical, poetic sections of the book, and Wellhausen's belief that the Confessions, as the prophet's private prayers, were no part of his public ministry.[4]

The position of these scholars inevitably raises the question why these allegedly private transactions between Jeremiah and YHWH found their way into the canonical – by definition *public* – literature. Furthermore, affinities between the Confessions and other canonical literature suggest that the poems cannot be regarded as private compositions pure and simple; because they are like psalms of lament in particular, which occupied a place in the regular worship of Israel, they must bear some relationship, however defined, to the public national life.[5]

The first major attempt to articulate the nature of the relationship of the Confessions to laments was that of W. Baumgartner, though he drew on the form-critical postulates of H. Gunkel.[6] He believed that Jeremiah knew and used the form-critical category of lament, but that he did so with variations which were characteristically prophetic. (Je. 11:18, for example, bespoke an audition of the prophet, understandable in the light of what we know from elsewhere in the prophecy, and without strict parallel in the laments.)[7] Baumgartner, however, did not move decisively away from the psychologizing interpretation typical of his period. The Confessions are still essentially prayers of the prophet, evidence of his outstanding 'sensitivity', and congruent with the alleged rise of religious individualism around the time of the exile.[8] Baumgartner thus highlighted the problem of the relation of the Confessions to the public life of Israel, and implicitly to the book of *Jeremiah*, but shrank back from a satisfying answer into the doctrine of religious individualism.

The affinities between the Confessions and the laments were capable, however, of bearing an interpretation which was wholly different, and indeed quite the reverse, as was demonstrated by H. Graf Reventlow. Reventlow denied that there were any features of the Confessions which could not be regarded as having their home in public, cultic settings. According to his study of the 'prophetic "I"', the prophet belongs to the class of cultic prophets, and his utterances are not his own, but are made for and on behalf of the cultic community. Reventlow's treatment is a systematic challenge to what he saw as the prevailing psychologizing approach to Jeremiah, bolstered by form-criticism from Gunkel to Westermann,[9] which had too narrow an understanding of prophetic forms (limited essentially to the 'word of judgment'), and thus allowed much other material to be seen as the prophet's own reflection.[10] Baumgartner, and also von Rad,[11] did not avoid Reventlow's criticism.

Reventlow's great advance over previous criticism was his attempt to answer the question about the setting of the Confessions in the life of Israel. In doing so he posed awkward questions to time-honoured conceptions about the nature of prophecy, and indeed challenged what had become the primary diagnostic weapon in the armoury of critics of Jeremiah, the prose-poetry distinction. This advance, however, was made at the expense of the personality of Jeremiah, which on his view is actually as much in the background as it was formerly in the foreground. Developments after Reventlow have been of two sorts, the one taking issue with his obscuring of the prophet's individuality, and the other supporting his interest, along different lines, in the contexting of the Confessions in *Jeremiah*.

Interest in the prophet as an individual was revived by U. Mauser, in a way which was not a simple reversion to the psychologizing interpretation of a former period. Mauser, in a treatment of Hosea, Jeremiah and Jesus, used the term *Menschwerdung* (incarnation) to characterize the role of the prophet in relation to the deity. In Hosea, Mauser adduces a number of contrasting utterances of YHWH (*e.g.* 9:15 and 14:5; 5:10 and 11:9; 4:6 and 11:8),[12] and argues that they represent real agony and change in his mind. The prophet then becomes God's 'image' (*Gottesbild*) inasmuch as he reflects YHWH's state of mind. Whereas Moses had mediated his favour, Hosea begins to mediate his wrath,[13] and the inner turmoil which goes with it. Hosea's marriage to a harlot is an obvious dimension of this. Hosea 9 goes further by revealing the prophet's own distress that comes in consequence of his prophetic office. The passage 9:7–8 begins to point towards the kind of protest more commonly associated with Jeremiah, and verse 14 has overtones of the later prophet's prayers for punishment on the people.[14]

In carrying the argument into Jeremiah, Mauser takes issue directly with Reventlow, claiming that the use of cultic forms does not diminish or preclude the real experience of the individual who uses them. The book of *Jeremiah*, on the contrary, is the classic case of a *Gottesgeschichte* (history of God – implying his thesis that God does change and suffer) paralleled by a *Prophetengeschichte* (history of a prophet).[15] The portrayal of Jeremiah, by his utterances and by the account of his experiences, becomes a paradigm of the life of YHWH with his people.[16] This view is clearly different from the psychologizing of Skinner. The life of Jeremiah, furthermore, is much more than a 'biography', told for purposes of pious modelling. And the prophet's expressions of distress are now seen in a quite different light.

The relationship between word of YHWH and words of the prophet was thus shown by Mauser to be far more complex than previous studies had believed. One potentially perplexing feature of the book's utterances illustrates the point. There are a number of passages in which it is difficult or impossible to know whether it is YHWH or the prophet who is speaking. The section 8:22 – 9:2, for example, is initially, to all appearances, the words of Jeremiah. While either he or YHWH might reasonably refer to Judah as 'my people' (22), it is more natural to think of Jeremiah weeping and going into the desert away from them. Yet the passage ends surprisingly with the words: 'and they do not know me, says the LORD'. This has led some commentators to emend in order to produce a

65

smoother sense.[17] The passage seems well designed, however, precisely to prompt a re-evaluation, in the light of the
final line, of its whole intent, and to divert the attention from
the suffering of the prophet to that of YHWH. The passage
4:19–22 has an exactly analogous movement, where the
phrase 'For my people are foolish, they know me not . . .' (22)
both accuses the people of a failure to understand YHWH,
and makes that failure the ground of a suffering which is to
all appearances Jeremiah's. Once again the suffering of
YHWH has been surprisingly evoked, by way of an astonish-
ingly bold anthropomorphism supplied by the experience of
the prophet.

The same point is somewhat differently illustrated by the
collocation 11:18–23; 12:1–6, 7–13, in which the treachery
of Jeremiah's 'house' (his family and the people of Anathoth)
is exhibited (11:21–23; 12:6), and made to lead into
YHWH's lament: 'I have forsaken my house.' In this case the
analogy between YHWH's experience and Jeremiah's is
effected by means of a paralleling of vocabulary and ideas.

YHWH's anger is anguished because he loves Judah. They
are his heritage, 'the beloved of my soul' (12:7). Similarly
Jeremiah is deeply attached to 'his' people (notice his
'mourning' for them because of their suffering, 8:18–21), yet
also expresses anger because of their sin (15:17). The analogy between the prophet and his God extends further, however, to register the scorn felt by the people for YHWH. The
people's contempt for Jeremiah needs no demonstration. Its
transfer to YHWH is already implied in 11:18 – 12:13, and is
clear in, for example, 6:10; 12:8b; 14:8.

It follows from the understanding of Jeremiah's role
which Mauser thus advocates that the prophet's life and
experience have a function in his proclamation. Life and
word mesh in his ministry. Both in his speech and in himself
he sets YHWH forth. The view outlined thus does better
justice to the question why these prayers have become part of
a public, canonical work than any 'private', psychologizing
interpretation could do (even if the manner in which the
words were delivered remains obscure). The force of this

proclamation is that YHWH suffers an inner tension because of his need to punish the people that he has chosen and loves. That tension is resolved in a triumph of love over anger (31:20 – a passage very like the similar resolution in Ho. 11:8–9). There is no direct analogy to this in the life of Jeremiah. Yet it relates to it in a different way, as we shall see.

It may be objected at this point that the view of Jeremiah thus sketched extinguishes the personality of Jeremiah just as surely as Reventlow did. Rightly understood, however, the contrary is the case. The validity of the proclamation depends precisely on the reality of the experience of the prophet. When Jeremiah expresses his own anguish, and we realize with a jolt that he is pointing more profoundly to a suffering of YHWH's (as in 4:19–22 and 8:22 – 9:2), the effect depends on the reality of the suffering of the human being who makes an impact – directly or indirectly – on the senses and compassion of his hearers or readers. The point has been cogently made by T. Polk.

Polk distinguishes between representation as 'sign' and as 'symbol'. The former characterizes a view of representation like Reventlow's, where the '"I" is of no significance in itself but is merely regarded as the "we" it represents'. In symbolic representation, in contrast, the 'I' can stand only for others by virtue of being fully itself.

> Thus the representative 'I' requires and trades on the individual 'I' for its intelligibility. The latter is present whenever the former occurs.[18]

Polk argues that this understanding is typically biblical, citing the eponymous Jacob as an additional example, who, in the roundness of his character, *is* Israel, rather than merely pointing to an entity that is entirely beyond himself. He goes on, furthermore, to interpret *Jeremiah* 14:1 – 15:4[19] in a manner which takes issue with Reventlow's attempt to subsume the whole under the category of lament, showing rather that the prophet sustains a dialogue with the people. (He thus affirms, for example, the integrity of 14:1, which

Reventlow had disallowed.)[20] Where there *is* a lament of the people (7–9), it is in fact insincere, and Jeremiah uses it to criticize that insincerity, which is in turn the ground of the prohibition of intercession in 14:11–12.[21]

According to this interpretation the utterances in 14:7–9, 19–22 are highly complex. They are on the one hand ironic statements in the mouth of the people. As such they fail to realize the devastating consequences, against a background of covenant theology, of seeking the presence of YHWH when they have failed to honour their covenant commitments. On the other, they are words of Jeremiah himself, by virtue of his (symbolic) representative capacity, and convey his own perplexity before the imminent judgment of YHWH, which he himself will also endure. This actual perplexity of the prophet, even as he conducts a critique of sinful Judah, carries over into the Confessions. Specifically, 15:5–21 resolves the tension in him that has reached a climax in 15:1–4, coming at last to personal words of reassurance in verses 19–21.[22] Jeremiah's representative prophetic role thus forces him into a relationship with his ministry which issues in the protest of the Confessions, and indeed in the words of assurance which come in their train. These will in turn come also to Judah, especially in 30–33 (with 15:19 *cf.* 31:20, on which see further below), and the result is to cast Jeremiah in a kind of 'servant' role.

The result of the work of Mauser and Polk is to set a new premium on the role of the prophet over against the rest of the community. In speaking YHWH's word he 'images' him among the people, with all the distancing from them which this entails. Yet he also hears the same word from the side of the people. There is therefore an 'imaging' of the people as well. (Note 15:16, the only place in the Old Testament where the 'proclaiming of YHWH's name' is related specifically to an individual as opposed to the whole people.)[23] One consequence is a participation in their suffering, and in a sense his expressions of perplexity are spoken on their behalf. They have, however, the further function of marking Jeremiah as one who can be addressed *qua* the people.

The Confessions in context

In considering Polk's treatment of *Jeremiah* 14 – 15 we have already broached the second development beyond Reventlow mentioned above, namely the contexting of the Confessions in the book, and particularly in *Jeremiah* 11 – 20. We have argued that hope for Judah is deliberately closed down in the flow of *Jeremiah* 11 – 20. Yet it is clear from what we have now seen of the role of the prophet *vis-à-vis* Judah that our earlier conclusion could be only provisional, pending a consideration of the way in which the prophet represents the people. That is to say, the relationship of Jeremiah to Judah is not exhausted by his addressing to them words of judgment, not even when these are reinforced by symbolic acts such as the breaking of the earthen flask (19:10). Alongside the dialogue between YHWH and Judah through Jeremiah, there is a dialogue between YHWH and Jeremiah himself. We have observed this dialogue in *Jeremiah* 14 – 15, in which Jeremiah looks to YHWH for deliverance (14:22), and receives in the end an assurance of it (15:19). If that assurance relates in the first instance to a deliverance of Jeremiah from his enemies within the people, it has overtones too of a deliverance of the nation from its enemies by virtue of the representative role of the prophet established in the dialogues of chapters 14 – 15.

Is there, then, hope for Judah in *Jeremiah* 1 – 20 by virtue of the representative role of Jeremiah? The question can be addressed by asking whether any trend is discernible in the statements of and to Jeremiah in the Confessions, both as a body of texts which naturally belong together and with regard to their context in *Jeremiah* 11 – 20. Attempts have been made to do this in considerable detail.[24]

There remains, however, a problem of method. When we speak of a trend, do we mean one that can be traced against the background of the course of the prophet's life? Do we mean a trend in terms of a traceable development in known forms? Or do we simply mean a development on the literary plane, an arrangement of the material in such a way as to serve a purpose in the discourse of the book as it unfolds? It will be apparent by now that definitions of the task in terms of the first two questions are highly problematical. Individual Confessions are not easily matched with times and places in the prophet's life, however much they ring true in terms of the general tenor of it as it is presented to us. And Reventlow's attempt at rigid formal classification of the Confessions in terms of the lament has failed to establish itself, as more recent studies have moved, in their different ways, towards asserting their freedom *vis-à-vis* the form.[25]

Nevertheless, variety still prevails in attempts to find order among the Confessions and in their relationship with their context. Ittmann's claim concerning their freedom from the lament rests on the belief that the lament itself has no fixed form in the Old Testament. The Confessions constitute a particular form of the lament, which draws also on other biblical antecedents, but is unique in prophecy.[26] He adopts a method, however, which depends for all that on the identification of an original Confessions form. The elements of this are (i) a description of the prophet's situation, (ii) an expression of trust in YHWH, with an appeal for deliverance, and (iii) YHWH's reaction. This form he then finds to be most fully present in 11:18–23; 12:1–6 and 18:18–22 (or rather the core of these, identified by literary critical analysis), among which he also finds vocabulary parallels.[27] The remaining Confessions then exhibit various degrees of breakdown in the form. Sections 15:15–20 and 20:7–9 have a new problematic, and are too revolutionary to press into any kind of form, while 17:14–18 stands even further from the original.[28]

The problem with Ittmann's reconstruction is its ambivalence regarding the heuristic status of form-criticism for the Confessions. His belief that there is a basic form which ultimately breaks down under the pressure of the subject-matter compromises the postulate of a basic form at all, whose features are in reality identified under the pressure of the analogy with the lament rather than the influence of the context. He fails in the end to decide between an approach that is either consistently form-orientated or consistently context-orientated. Implicit in his method, furthermore, are assumptions of a biographical nature about the prophet.

Diamond's approach, in contrast, is firmly context-orientated. Equally convinced that the Confessions are independent of the lament, yet properly reticent about their relation to Jeremiah's life, he argues for an editorial arrangement of the Confessions in relation to each other and to their context. He discovers two separate cycles of Confessions. The first consists of those in chapters 11, 12 and 15, in which the prophet confronts YHWH about the nature of his ministry. The second cycle, in 18:18 – 20:13, features a clash between Jeremiah and his opponents over their failure to respond to YHWH's word. The passage 17:14–18 is transitional between the two, and 20:14–18 lies outside the two cycles and is properly a self-curse. Together with verses 7–13, it resolves issues in the two cycles, mirroring the progress within them.[29]

The individual Confessions are well integrated into their contexts, in chapters 11 – 13, 14 – 17, 18 – 20. The connecting idea, that gives sense to the corpus, is that of theodicy. The Confessions, indeed,

> provide a concrete illustration of the nation's apostasy, witnessing to the national refusal to heed the divine word; thus the Confessions are an integral part of the development of a theodicy.[30]

On this view the confrontation between Jeremiah and YHWH becomes a mere undercurrent in the Confessions. The significance of the two cycles is that the prophet's questioning of his office is answered by its confirmation. The real issue can then be pursued, namely the people's rejection of the word of YHWH through his spokesman.[31]

It is clear how this understanding of the Confessions sits well with our interpretation of *Jeremiah* 11 – 20 as a demonstration of the closing down of hope for Judah. By

Diamond's account the Confessions serve the very same purpose. Yet his relegation of the prophet's 'suffering servant' role to the status of a sub-theme is unsatisfying. He sees Jeremiah's lament-like speeches on behalf of the people in *Jeremiah* 14 as an attempt by the prophet to exercise a cultic-mediatorial role in keeping with the expectations of the people, and indeed the salvation-prophets.[32] The outcome of the attempt, however, is to silence it. 'Jeremiah is to be permitted one role in relation to the nation – that of opposition . . .'[33]

Such a view, however, not only does little justice to the renewed, even heightened, burst of perplexity which emanates from Jeremiah in chapter 20, but seriously underestimates his representative capacity, as we have seen it in our discussion of Polk and Mauser. Polk, following Gerstenberger, points out that the rejection of Jeremiah's intercession in 15:1 is not the end of the story of his representation of the people. The end of this particular drama is actually at 15:21, with its promise of salvation.[34] And Jeremiah's representative role, far from being diminished, is actually expanded; if he cannot represent the people by interceding, he will now represent them with his life, 'both in what he suffers and in what he is promised'.[35]

The figure of Jeremiah, especially in the Confessions – though they can be rightly understood only in their general context in the book – is, therefore, extremely complex. At once, he represents the people, he represents YHWH, and he remains himself. It follows that nearly all the words he utters, in those sections where his representative role is most in evidence, are complex. In 14:19–22, for example, he speaks for the people. In doing so he cannot but evoke their failure to take the prayer to themselves in any genuine way. His words, therefore, are a kind of criticism of the nation, sealing their fate. At the same time, they are words which he, Jeremiah, *does* sincerely take on his own lips. By virtue of his representative role, therefore, the prayer becomes, after all, a genuine prayer of the people. Their participation in the prayer, however, with the hope of salvation to which it gives rise, is secured only through the prophet. This is the subject of *Jeremiah* 15.

At the close of chapter 15 Jeremiah is given a word of assurance. This word addressed *to* the prophet is as complex as the words uttered by him. Here, the significance of the word of assurance is not limited to the prophet alone. It finds a 'fuller sense', as it were, in its reiteration in 31:20 to the whole people. In the Confessions therefore, Jeremiah has become the bearer of the nation's hope of salvation.[36]

The complexity of the figure of Jeremiah does not end there. Though he represents Judah, and there is a sense in which this makes him a kind of model of obedience and prayerfulness, his individuality comes through in his inclination to throw off the burdens of his calling. In the midst of his representative role he can still be distinguished from the people, as in his expressed feelings of isolation and anger with them. His frustration is exemplified in 15:10–12, and comes to a head in 20:7–12, in the course of which he seems to admit that he has repeatedly tried to refrain from prophesying (8). For this reason he can be rebuked, and recalled to his duty (12:5–6; 15:19–21). Even here, however, Jeremiah's fractiousness is not a thing in itself. It too corresponds to something in the life of Judah, namely her reluctance to shoulder the responsibility of her own 'vocation' as the elect of YHWH. Jeremiah's very reluctance thus has a positive role, namely to occasion the words of rebuke, which also carry with them words of promise.

It remains to consider how the evaluation thus offered is affected by the last of the Confessions, 20:7–13, 14–18. These passages are perhaps the darkest of all Jeremiah's outpourings, and they have proved troublesome to those who have tried to find patterns in the development of the Confessions.[37] Von Rad's judgment that the Confessions merely seem to subside further and further into despair appears justified by the tones found here.[38] In particular, 20:14–18 is ominous because of the shift from mere complaint to something like self-curse, the epitome of word-rejection because it denies the very act of creation, let alone vocation and salvation. These verses, furthermore, as has been well observed, occupy a position of importance in the structure and theology of the whole to this point[39] and beyond.[40] And there appears to be no answer to relieve the gloom, as there was in chapters 12 and 15.

The problem of 20:14–18 is as much a problem about *Jeremiah* 11 – 20 as a whole as about the Confessions in particular. We have found evidence to suggest that a dominant thrust of 11 – 20 is the closing down of hope. We have now seen, however, that that evaluation has to be qualified by the fact that Jeremiah, as a representative of Judah, is made to carry hope for the nation in his own person. The question arises, consequently, how that hope is conveyed in and through chapter 20.

The answer is not difficult regarding 20:7–13. The complaint that YHWH has deceived Jeremiah (*pittâ*, 20:7), broached in 15:18 (*'akzāḇ*, a deceitful brook), becomes full-orbed here. It echoes a complaint made in an earlier part of the book (4:10, *hiššeh*, deceive), however, where it is said to be a deception, not of the prophet but of the people. Though the vocabulary changes, the accusation unmistakably recurs, therefore, where the deception of the people is evoked by that of Jeremiah. A further link between prophet and people is forged by the immediate context. When Jeremiah hears whispering ('Terror is on every side!'), he uses the same term (*māḡôr missāḇîḇ*) with which he has renamed his tormentor Pashhur in 20:3. These echoes remind us that Judah's fate is at issue in this complaint too. Though we never lose sight of Jeremiah here (in his compulsion to speak the word, for example), there is in YHWH's prevailing over Jeremiah an echo of his prevailing over Judah which will lead to exile (note the analogy in 20:16; *cf.* 4:7b). On the other hand, the adversaries who wait to pounce on Jeremiah point too readily beyond themselves to the captors who will carry off the people.

This complaint has an optimistic outcome, however, well in keeping with many of the psalms of lament. Jeremiah's persecutors will stumble before the might of YHWH the holy warrior (11), just as Babylon will fall later to the same foe (note the military imagery in *e.g.* 50:25, 35–38; 51:20–23, and *passim* in 50–51). And the cry of praise in verse 13 signals the certainty that such vengeance will indeed come.[41]

It is 20:14–18 which poses a stiffer problem. Following directly on the certainty of a hearing (verse 13), it depicts Jeremiah in the greatest despair yet, a mood from which there is apparently no egress. Yet its starkness is itself a key to the structure of the book. The solution to the problem lies, as has been shown by Clines-Gunn and others, in the fact that the impassioned cry of 20:18 not only resonates with *Jeremiah* 1, where the answer has been given in advance, but it calls forth the entire remainder of the book after this point, which is also in its own way an answer to the same question. Jeremiah was born precisely to undertake the critique of the nation's mores which is depicted there in his confrontations with the political leadership.[42]

The depth of the darkness here, however, has a further dimension, which relates to Jeremiah's representative role. The depiction of a death of Jeremiah, or more precisely of his never having been, raises also the possibility of a death of Judah, or perhaps a never having been. The passage is a graphic way of asking, what is the *raison d'être* of Judah itself? The answer will consist partly in that prophetic critique of the nation in all its political and moral roundness, which will be the subject of much that follows. It will also consist, however, in the announcement of a new future for the nation, based on a whole new approach on YHWH's part to the covenant relationship.

The close of *Jeremiah* 11 – 20 is therefore both heavily ironic and poetically appropriate. On one level, the curtain is now certain to fall on the act in Judah's history known as monarchy. The inevitability of that scenario is reinforced by the writing out of the kings, the last king 'Zedekiah' occupying centre stage in the chapters that follow (21–24). Judah's God, who fought for her ancestors, is now set against her in a reversal of the holy war, the only possible outcome being the 'death' of exile. On another level, the survival of Judah is already secured by the representative role of Jeremiah, developed in the agonies of the Confessions, by reason of the assurances made to him there. As Jeremiah will survive, so will Judah. The ironies of his compatriots' attempts to do away with him are glaring in the face of his actual role. Those ironies will have ample scope for development in the remainder of the story.

Conclusions

In the present chapter we have argued that the figure of the prophet in *Jeremiah* is neither merely an example of an individual's great personal piety, nor a detached cultic functionary. Rather, there is an incarnational aspect to his role, by which he embodies both the experience of the people and that of YHWH, yet without ever ceasing to be an individual personality. This portrayal of the prophet has as its framework, and in turn helps create, the idea of hope for Judah that lies through and beyond suffering.

The prophetic model found in *Jeremiah* is not simply identical with the conception of prophecy in DtH. This is not to say that it is at odds with such an understanding; on the contrary, the clashes between Jeremiah and the salvation-prophets must be understood partly in terms of the criteria of authenticity laid down in Deuteronomy 18:20–22.[43] Nevertheless the figure of Jeremiah belongs in a sophisticated way to the theological problematic of *Jeremiah* itself.

It is mistaken, therefore, to expect to find in *Jeremiah* a normative view of prophecy provided by DtH. Carroll, for example, sees the motif of prophet as intercessor as Deuteronomistic (citing 1 Sa. 12:23). The analogy is fair enough in itself. Yet when the figure of the prophet becomes complex, Carroll treats this as an aspect of the complexity which he sees in the growth of the Jeremiah tradition. He writes:

Whether the overlapping motifs of national lament bewailing the exile and the prophet as persecuted figure and representative figure of the community come from different stages of the redaction or belong to different groups (different groups of deuteronomists or deuteronomists and non-deuteronomists?) cannot be determined with any certainty. All that may be said with any certitude is that the redaction of the Jeremiah tradition was an extremely complex affair.[44]

This passage illustrates very well the inadequacy of the 'Deuteronomistic' idea for understanding *Jeremiah*, and the likelihood of being misled by using it as a key to interpreting *Jeremiah*. In fact Carroll's 'overlapping motifs' can be accommodated within the sophisticated portrayal of the prophet which we have tried to uncover.

The same point can be made in reply to McKane. McKane (criticizing Reventlow) recognizes that the distinction between Jeremiah as a private individual and as a 'representative, communal intercessor' is a false one, and therefore acknowledges the complexity of the figure in the book. Nevertheless, he argues on the one hand that 15:10–11 (12) and 15:15–21 are expressions of private anguish, and on the other he denies to Jeremiah the 'communal laments', 14:2–10; 14:17 – 15:4.[45] With regard to the latter he finds it 'difficult to believe that Jeremiah would have identified himself with a theology whose climax was a *šālôm* oracle, or would have offered a prayer which he knew to rest on a foundation of *šeqer*' – *šeqer* being understood as a deep falsehood in the life of the people.[46] Here too, I think, the portrayal of Jeremiah is in reality more complex than has been allowed. As far as the element of reassurance is concerned, especially in 15:19–21, I have argued that the word to Jeremiah functions ultimately in relation to the whole community. (Jeremiah's transformation into a salvation-prophet is also discussed further below, in chapter 4.) At this point as elsewhere, therefore, McKane's belief in a

'D. redaction'[47] consisting of fundamentally disparate small units has led him, in my view, to do too little justice to sustained thematic continuities in the book. In the present chapter, I hope we have seen in particular that the portrayal of the prophet, like other aspects of the book, cannot be labelled Deuteronomistic, but is specifically Jeremianic.[48]

CHAPTER FOUR

The revival of hope (25 – 36)

The structure of *Jeremiah* 25 – 45

We have now seen how the first part of *Jeremiah* (1 – 24) was a demonstration that there could be no hope of salvation for Judah except through the judgment of exile. The second part of the book will concentrate on what lies beyond exile, and in it hope for the future is opened up in a new way. Before observing how this is achieved, we must spend a moment considering the structure of chapters 25 – 45. This is because their structure is not immediately obvious, and different accounts of it have been offered. Chapter 25 illustrates the point at the outset.

In the MT,[1] chapter 25 is clearly, at one level, an independent unit, marked out by its theme of YHWH's judgment on the nations, beginning with Judah, and ending with Babylon. It could be read, however, either as the conclusion to the first part of the book (thus 1–25), or as an introduction to the second (thus 25–45). Holladay, for example, takes the first option, dividing his commentary after chapter 25,[2] while others prefer the latter.[3] There are in fact, as we shall see, good reasons for both these views, and it seems best to regard the chapter as forming a link between the two parts of the book.

Chapters 26 – 45 represent the bulk of the second part of *Jeremiah*. A decision about the structure of these is complicated also. We shall proceed step by step. First, chapters 26 – 29 form a fairly obvious unit, because of their focus on the theme of opposition to Jeremiah's prophecy, both from the leadership and the populace (26), and specifically from other prophets (28–29). Second, chapters 30 – 33 possess a clear unity of theme, namely the salvation of the covenant people, for which reason these chapters have come to be known as the 'Book of Consolation'. These two sections, incidentally, are linked to each other in ways which we shall observe.

As chapters 34 – 36 are the most difficult to assign in a structural analysis of the second part of the book, we shall move next to chapters 37 – 44. These chapters are widely regarded as a unit because of their unity of theme, namely the story of the last days of Judah, its fall, and the aftermath both in Palestine and in Egypt.[4] Chapter 45 stands aside somewhat both from 37 – 44 and from the oracles against the nations which follow, being a word from YHWH expressly for Baruch. It is sometimes included with 37 – 44, on the grounds of obvious connections with chapter 36 (cf. 36:1–4; 45:1). Yet equally, it serves as a prelude to the oracles against the nations, because of the words 'behold, I am bringing evil upon all flesh' (5). It should also be noted that the new set of oracles which begins at chapter 46 is entrusted to Seraiah, Baruch's brother, for deliverance in Babylon (51:59). It is not given to Baruch to go to the centre of Empire; he must rather accompany his reluctant master to Egypt. Chapter 45, together with the notice in 51:59, seems to acknowledge that Baruch has bowed out of the action at his due moment. The connection between the passages forges another link between 45 and 46 – 51. Chapter 45, therefore, can be linked both with what precedes it and with what follows it. It is similar in this respect to chapter 25.

Only chapters 34 – 36 remain to be considered, other sections having been identified around them. They are not in themselves an obvious unity, dealing as they do with different periods in Jeremiah's life. They do, however, have a certain unity of theme, namely the resistance of the people to the word of YHWH, focused in that of the Davidic dynasty. (That this is true of chapter 35 will emerge from our interpretation of it.) The larger question about these chapters is

80

whether they belong with 26 – 33, as a conclusion, or with 37 – 45, as an introduction. That they belong with the preceding material is widely held, for good reasons. In particular, extensive similarities between chapters 26 and 36 have been noticed, which suggest that they are the beginning and end respectively of a subsection of the book.[5] In addition, 34:1–5 can be seen as a reprise, with some development, of 32:1–5,[6] suggesting a connection in thought between the 'Book of Consolation' and chapter 34.

On the other hand, there is an unmistakable change of tone with chapter 34. The 'Book of Consolation' was devoted to oracles of salvation, and indeed the salvation theme, as we shall see, has been in preparation well before it (arguably since chapter 25). Yet now the note of judgment because of word-rejection supervenes once more, and will be sustained until chapter 44. In this sense, therefore, 34 – 36 can well be read as a prelude to the story of the last days of Judah and beyond (37 – 44). Chapters 34 – 36 (like chapters 25 and 45) are both retrospective and prospective.

The foregoing skeleton of the structure of *Jeremiah* 25 – 45 will be given flesh in the more extended interpretation which follows. We may note at this point, however, that there can be no hard and fast analysis of the book. This observation is consistent with our view that the book as it stands is a thought-out composition of the elements that comprise it. Analyses which claim to have more definitely identified components of the book are often conducted as attempts to trace the story of its growth. I shall not try to do that here, mainly because I think that such attempts meet with rather limited success.

The foregoing discussion results in an analysis of 25 – 45 which could be expressed as follows: 25; 26 – (33)36; (34)37 – 44; 45.

The revival of hope in *Jeremiah*

We have seen in our study of *Jeremiah* 1 – 24 that the main thrust of that section was to show why exile became inevitable for Judah, namely because of her chronic persistence in rebellion against YHWH. To this extent its theology was like that of DtH, a theodicy which justified YHWH in his decision to let his wrath fall on his covenant people. DtH had left open the possibility of YHWH's future intervention in principle, but had not developed a theology of hope involving a return to the land.[7] *Jeremiah* 1–24 has begun to go beyond DtH, both in its adumbration of a purpose of YHWH for Judah *by means of* the exile (Je. 24), a purpose which *did* involve return to the land, and in the figure of Jeremiah, who though proclaiming disaster and articulating the despair of Judah in his own experience, bears their hopes for the future in his person. Already, therefore, we have begun to see how *Jeremiah* marks an advance over DtH in its interpretation of Deuteronomy. *Jeremiah* 24:7, indeed, picks up a feature of Deuteronomy 30 which we noticed DtH did not, namely the idea of YHWH's own creation of a capacity in his people to obey him. Deuteronomy 30:6 uses the metaphor of circumcision of the heart to introduce the idea. (It had also appeared at Dt. 10:16 in the form of an exhortation, but that exhortation is overtaken within Dt. by the recognition of Israel's incapacity to obey. Dt. 30:6, therefore, functions within Dt. to resolve a tension which is addressed in that book, namely how Israel might be faithful to the covenant.)

As we thus observe similarities between *Jeremiah* and Deuteronomy, it becomes clear that the question whether *Jeremiah* is 'Deuteronomic' can mask a question about the relation between Deuteronomy and DtH. Deuteronomy and DtH do not, in fact, speak univocally about the future hope of Israel (as a comparison of Dt. 30:1–6 and 1 Ki. 8:46–53 in particular shows).[8] The relation of *Jeremiah* to the 'Deuteronomistic' literature, therefore, is not simple, but part of a wide range of issues of interpretation. The point is nowhere more sharply evident than in relation to the topic of hope for the future. As we shall see, *Jeremiah* interacts both with DtH (in relation to Josiah) and with Deuteronomy itself.

Regarding hope, *Jeremiah* mirrors the train of thought we

have just observed in Deuteronomy. It too introduces the metaphor of circumcision of the heart by way of exhortation (4:4), an exhortation which cannot meet an adequate response. The metaphor returns in 9:24, no longer as an exhortation but as part of the picture of an apostate nation. It does not return again in the book. Strictly, therefore, Deuteronomy's use of the metaphor is not followed; Jeremiah adopts it in an individual way. Nevertheless, *Jeremiah* does continue the thought of Deuteronomy, in 24:7:

> 'I will give them a heart to know that I am the LORD; and they shall be my people and I will be their God, for they shall return to me with their whole heart.'

Nor is this a mere assent in *Jeremiah* to the theological proposition of Deuteronomy, which in that book was left undeveloped. Rather it marks the beginning of reflection on it which will be the main substance of *Jeremiah* from this point through its next major section, ending at chapter 36. The orientation of *Jeremiah* to Deuteronomy 30 is proved by a further point of contact, namely the phrase, 'then the LORD your God will restore your fortunes' ($w^e\check{s}\bar{a}\underline{b}$ ... '$e\underline{t}$ $\check{s}^e\underline{b}\hat{u}\underline{t}^e\underline{k}\bar{a}$). This phrase, used only here in Deuteronomy 30:3, occurs, with slight variants, eleven times in *Jeremiah*, eight referring to the restoration of Judah.[9] Once again *Jeremiah* has taken its cue from Deuteronomy, but, as we shall see, develops the idea in its own way. It forms a part, nevertheless, of the general pursuit in *Jeremiah* of the theology of a restoration of Israel/Judah. This restoration embraces, but is more than, a physical return to the land, being above all a restitution of the people as a faithful covenant partner.

We are ready now to turn to our interpretation of the second part of *Jeremiah*. In the remainder of the present chapter we address *Jeremiah* 25 – 36.

Jeremiah 25

As we have seen, chapter 25 stands at an important juncture in the book. There are several indications of this. First, Jeremiah offers a retrospect on his ministry to date, mentioning the period of twenty-three years since his call during which he has prophesied continuously (3). The information is remarkable if only because it is unique in the book, and in Old Testament prophecy. It is possible that some or all of 25:1–14 accompanied, either as prologue or epilogue,[10] the first scroll of Jeremiah's prophecies read to Jehoiakim in the fourth year of his reign (36:1; cf. 25:1). The effect of Jeremiah's review of his ministry in this way is to focus on his prophetic role. That role is made prominent at this juncture in the first instance to reiterate the accusation that Judah has not obeyed the word of YHWH. In making the point our passage echoes the terms of 2 Kings 17, especially in the phrase, 'although the LORD persistently sent to you all his servants the prophets' (4; cf. 2 Ki. 17:13).

The allusion to that chapter in this is in fact complex. There as here, the definitive failure of Israel/Judah to hear the prophets is connected with the theme of the nations (gôyim), with which the covenant people now seems to be progressively aligned (cf. above on the gôyim theme in Je. 1 – 20), at the cost of her privileged status. The threat of loss of land is as radical as that: it means an undoing of election itself. The point is emphasized even more heavily in Jeremiah 27, where the mission of Nebuchadrezzar is directed against nations in general, in a way which classes Judah along with them, and implicitly calls her future into question. To this extent the gôyim motif in Jeremiah 25 and 27 strikes similar chords to those struck by the Kings passage. In Jeremiah, however, while it continues a thrust which was prominent in chapters 1 – 20, it becomes essentially a background for more positive reflection on Judah's future – which was by no means the case in Kings.

The second important feature of Jeremiah 25 is its introduction (12) of Jeremiah's prediction of the seventy-year duration of the exile. By virtue of this prediction, the present passage is directly continuous with 21:8–11 and chapter 24. Like them, it formalizes the contention that there can no longer be effective repentance on Judah's part into a revelation of the future. The former passages showed that YHWH had plans for those who would undergo the exile; the present one assumes that, and goes on to specify how long it would last. This has the dual function of showing that the exile is no negligible thing, as some will argue against Jeremiah, and of encouraging those who would be exiled with the knowledge that there would be an end to their alienation.

Third, the picture of Judah restored is completed by the corresponding picture of Babylon discomfited (12–13). The time of wrath for Judah[11] will soon give way to a time of salvation, and YHWH's anger will be turned against her tormentors, chiefly Babylon.

Finally, verses 15–38 have an obvious connection with the oracles against the nations. (They actually form a conclusion to them in LXX; 25:15–38 MT = 32:1–24 LXX.) They are not inappropriate in their present setting, however, forming a parallel to verses 1–14 in their portrayal of a judgment falling first on Judah and the nations around her *at the hands of* Babylon, then on Babylon herself (26).

The importance of *Jeremiah* 25 in the structuring of MT *Jeremiah* is clear. In one sense it functions to postpone the main section of oracles against the nations, so that it might fall in a more climactic position. But it also has its own rationale. It serves the purpose, to which *Jeremiah* 21 – 24 are also subject, of marking a turning point in the articulation of the message. As chapters 21 – 24 set the message in the context of its whole span by their orientation to the last Judean king, Zedekiah, so does chapter 25 by its adumbration of the downfall of Babylon. In the process, the note of hope for a future beyond exile, sounded in 21 – 24, gains some development. This development continues in *Jeremiah* 26 – 29.

Jeremiah 26 – 29

This section is dominated by three themes, all of them already familiar from 21 – 24 and 25, namely, the prophet and the prophetic word, the status of Judah as the people of YHWH, and restoration.

Jeremiah 26 focuses immediately on the prophetic word. The chapter serves not only to introduce the subject appropriately within 26 – 36 (where it will be echoed at the end of Jehoiakim's attempt to destroy the collection of Jeremiah's words)[12] but has a wider structural function by virtue of its echo of the Temple sermon of *Jeremiah* 7:1–15. It is probable that the two accounts relate to the same event in Jeremiah's ministry. We are not directly concerned so much with the question of relative originality as with the use made of the Temple sermon in developing the book's message. The Temple sermon had immense symbolic force in *Jeremiah* 1 – 20 because it showed that enmity against YHWH was right at the heart of the nation, even in the institutions which overtly proclaimed his name. It was thus central to the critique of Judah for her rejection of YHWH's word.

That critique is now deliberately revived by the repetition of the incident. Its relative brevity suggests a kind of resumptive character,[13] as if it can suppose that the argument is familiar. It is interesting that 26:1, in contrast to 7:1, does not even carry the name of Jeremiah. That can, no doubt, be taken for granted too. Yet the omission may be significant, announcing at the outset of both chapter and new section (26 – 36) that the subject at issue is the word, rather than the prophet for his own sake (thus against older understandings of the latter part of *Jeremiah* as a 'biography'). The function of the record of the sermon here is not to call the people to repentance in any simple sense. We know by now that that exhortation is deemed to have fallen on deaf ears, and that YHWH has other plans for doing his will in Judah. The sermon may rather be read as a record of what happened when the prophet preached. The account in this place is therefore one of those demonstrations of the hardness of

Judah's heart which is characteristic of the second part of the book. The change in mode which occurs at about this point in the book (from chiefly oracle to chiefly narrative) conforms to the purpose we have observed in the book on other grounds, namely to show that Judah could not or would not repent. The sermon is repeated in order to supply the story of how it was received, which was missing in *Jeremiah* 7.

The centrality of the word in the chapter is clear from three further features. The first is the mere repetition of words connected with 'word' (*dābār*, word; *dibber*, speak) and obedience or hearing, especially in verses 7–9. It appears to be the accumulation of this vocabulary which prompts the murderous reaction of 'the priests and the prophets and all the people', verse 8 (heavily ironic because of their failure to see that it is they who are in danger of death).

The second feature is the appeal by 'the princes and all the people' (12) (against the hawkish 'priests and prophets' – who were evidently most threatened by Jeremiah: the 'people' seem somewhat mobile in this account, as mobs are)[14] to the precedent of Micah of Moresheth. Micah's predicted destruction of Jerusalem had not come about, because Hezekiah had repented; their best plan would be to *hear* this prophet and do likewise. The advice was Gamaliel-like. It shows that the preaching of Jeremiah did provoke some constructive thinking and heart-searching in Judah. Yet it is not the decisive point in the chapter. It prevails only to the extent of rescuing Jeremiah from imminent death. The decisive response to Jeremiah's preaching comes in the treatment of the unfortunate Uriah.

Uriah enters the narrative only to meet his death. He is, as a prophet, in all important respects like Jeremiah (20). Unfortunately, however, he does not enjoy the same protection of friends at court. His death at the hands of the frustrated and vicious Jehoiakim shows that the king's real enmity is against the word of YHWH, and that it will manifest itself against any of its bearers. The story of Uriah is the third of those features which shows that it is the word itself which is at stake here. Jeremiah's survival ensures that that issue can be carried forward in what follows.

It should be clear from our discussion of *Jeremiah* 21 – 24 and 25 that the subject of prophecy has not been re-engaged in chapter 26 merely for the purpose of reiterating Judah's failure to hear it. We have been led to expect some more positive development. And this is indeed in store in the shape of Jeremiah's confrontation with the salvation-prophets. It is one thing to insist that Judah should have listened to YHWH's 'servants the prophets' (25:4); it is another to know who they are. Jeremiah has admittedly adopted ploys which were designed to demonstrate his own credibility. The appeal to the destruction of Shiloh, for example (7:14; 26:6), was intended to prove that a true prophet need not be a salvation-prophet.

Hananiah-ben-Azzur, however, is intent on proving the opposite. He is introduced (28:1) simply as a 'prophet'. There is no question, therefore, about his acceptance in that role. And he enters the scene with the express purpose of challenging Jeremiah. This he does by directly contradicting him on the matter of the Temple vessels, lately carried off to Babylon, and which Jeremiah has said will remain there indefinitely (27:22; 28:3). (Chronologically, then, we have moved on some years from the Temple sermon of chapter 26, which happened in the reign of Jehoiakim; the arrangement of material is clearly thematic here.) The phrasing of verse 5 ensures that we do not miss the element of confrontation in chapter 28: 'Then the prophet Jeremiah [as if we needed reminding that he was such] spoke to Hananiah the prophet ...' (*cf.* also 15). The vocabulary of prophecy abounds in the verses that follow, and Jeremiah appeals to the tradition of prophecy in which both he and Hananiah stand (8). The outcome of the confrontation is temporarily in doubt, even in Jeremiah's mind, it seems. In the end, however, Jeremiah successfully appeals to the criterion of vindication (verses 15–17; *cf.* Dt. 18:21–22 – which, of course, he had largely been unable to during the greater part of his ministry, because the exile had taken so long in coming). Even now, Jeremiah's appeal to Deuteronomy's criterion of vindication is no mere theological orthodoxy. *His* vindication has been, as it were, through fire, and comes to us as part of the highly sophisticated picture of the prophet who suffers the torment of self-doubt, which in turn embodies the torment of God.

If, furthermore, the confrontation with Hananiah originally had the purpose of vindicating Jeremiah, that is no longer strictly the purpose which it has in the book before us. For the readers of the book, Jeremiah already stands vindicated, because they know that his message has been borne out at last. The issue in *Jeremiah* 28, carried over into 29, is the transformation of Jeremiah into a salvation-prophet! And this cannot be done without a grand demonstration of the difference between *his* salvation-prophecy and that of those prophets who said that the exile would never come, or 'be over by Christmas'![15]

Accordingly, the transformation of Jeremiah into a prophet of hope is cautious, sustaining the critique of those salvation-prophets who resemble Hananiah, and who have even carried their interpretation of YHWH's intentions into exile. It is careful to maintain the doctrine that the exile will be lasting, by repeating the prediction of its seventy-year duration (10). The command to seek the welfare of Babylon, furthermore (7), arises from and supports the teaching that there is no future for Judah apart from exile, and certainly not by way of any premature return to the land lately forsaken (16–19). Nevertheless, the change of tone is real. No longer is there doubt concerning the future status of Judah. If she was classed ominously with the nations at large, a theme which had its climax as recently as chapter 27, YHWH now speaks reassuringly: 'For I know the plans I have for you, ... plans for welfare and not for evil, to give you a future and a hope' (11).

The change in this respect is echoed in the terms used for the nation. Throughout *Jeremiah* 27 and 28 it has been referred to by distancing and somewhat contemptuous expressions: 'your people' (*'ammekā*), addressed to Zedekiah, 27:13; 'all this people' (*kol-hā'ām hazzeh*), verse 16, *cf.* 28:1, 5, 7, 15. This has been something of a habit of speech throughout the prophecy, and it is dominant here as far as 29:32, where, however, it suddenly and triumphantly gives way to a re-adoption of the term 'my people' (*'ammî*) in the mouth of YHWH. Hitherto in the prophecy this particular expression has been used largely to emphasize the scandal of the fact that the people of YHWH have so utterly rebelled against him (*e.g.* 2:4, 13, 32 *etc.*). It is sometimes used to express the grief of YHWH (and Jeremiah) that the ordinary people have been systematically misled by their leaders and suffered as a result (*e.g.* 6:14; 8:11, 21–23). Within 1–20 the phrase is used in a statement of promise for Judah only at 12:14–16. The negative trend is properly arrested at 24:7, which affirms that a covenant will once again be made between YHWH and his people, in that programmatic vision which led into the present unpacking of the theme of hope. The declaration at 29:32, therefore, complements that vision in the context of the whole prophecy, even as it makes its own impact within its more immediate context. Henceforth, especially in the 'Book of Consolation', the covenant form will be freely used.

Other familiar strains are also put into reverse. If Jeremiah was formerly to refrain from marriage to show that it was not a time for the gladness that went with it, or even for giving birth to a new generation (16:2–3), the people are now exhorted to marry and multiply in the alien city (29:6). In Babylon too there will be 'welfare' (*šālôm*), verse 7. If the prophets whom Jeremiah opposed had promised *shalom* where there was none (6:14; 8:11), he now offers it in a realistic context: no *light* healing of the people's wound, rather one that comes in and through the purging of exile. (Notice that the condemnation of the falsehood [*šeqer*] of those prophets, 6:13; 8:10, is sustained here, 29:9, to reinforce the point that there remains no easy path to *shalom*.)

Finally, *Jeremiah* 29 initiates the transformation of the

theme of 'return'. We saw above (chapter 1) how the verb *šûḇ* was the subject of extensive word-plays designed to stress the people's incapacity to repent and her chronic tendency to apostasy. Now 29:14 sees the introduction of a new play on the same verb, which answers the problem posed by the former kind of usage, and which will become a refrain in the 'Book of Consolation'. The phrase in question is the promise of YHWH: 'I will restore your fortunes' (*wᵉšaḇtî 'etṧᵉḇîṯᵉḵem*). It will be immediately evident that the phrase not only makes a contrast with the hitherto prevailing kind of usage of *šûḇ* in the book (*e.g.* 3:12, 14), but it also forges a connection with Deuteronomy 30:3. We saw in our treatment of *Jeremiah* 24 (above, chapter 2) that that chapter had in common with the Deuteronomy passage its theology of a new initiative on YHWH's part in facilitating a renewed relationship between himself and his people. While the phrase 'I will restore your fortunes' did not occur in *Jeremiah* 24, it now does so, by way of a continuation of the theology which was perpetrated there. (There are clear echoes of 24:5–7 in 29:10–14.)

With the introduction of the phrase 'I will restore your fortunes' we have strong support for our contention that *Jeremiah* takes its cue from Deuteronomy 30, and indeed that its chief distinguishing feature *vis-à-vis* DtH is in its development of the theology that appeared baldly in that chapter. The phrase occurs seven times in the 'Book of Consolation' (30:3, 18; 31:23; 32:44; 33:7, 11, 26), typically in connection with language that draws on the election traditions of Israel (David and the patriarchs, 33:26, *cf.* 30:18; allusions to Zion-theology, 30:18; 31:23). The frequency of the expression in 30 – 33 suggests that Jeremiah's new-covenant theology, which gains its most extensive development in those chapters, is the main method adopted in the book for building on the foundation of Deuteronomy 30:3.

The 'Book of Consolation' (*Jeremiah* 30 – 33)

On any account of *Jeremiah*, chapters 30 – 33 mark themselves out as being somehow different from the rest. The
dominant note here is one of salvation, hence the use of the
term 'Book of Consolation' to characterize it. The phenomenon has been accounted for in various ways. Mowinckel,
for example, found it necessary to devise a separate source
(D) for (much of) 30 – 31, because they did not seem suitable
to the three main sources to which he believed the remainder
of the book could be assigned (A, B, C).[16] His source D
comprised preaching which Jeremiah had directed to the
former northern kingdom in his early ministry. We have
seen in our discussion of *Jeremiah* 3 how this idea has more
recently been followed by Holladay. We found cause to call it
into question, however, on the basis of our understanding of
the meaning of that passage as a whole.[17]

Similarly, our study of the present chapters can also be
pursued in terms of the structure and theology of the whole
book. Despite the new atmosphere, there remain many
points of contact between the prophecy up to this point and
these chapters. Indeed, it is our contention that the relationship between the 'Book of Consolation' and the rest of *Jeremiah* constitutes the distinctive theological contribution of
the work. The orientation towards *Israel* and Judah belongs
to the theology of new covenant, as we shall see.

First, the idea of YHWH's plans comes to fruition. That
idea was introduced in 23:20 in connection with the first
sustained encounter with the false prophets. Because the
latter had not 'stood in my council' (22) they could not know
YHWH's plans, and were able to continue with their misguided message of easy deliverance. The motif of YHWH's
plans recurs in 29:11, in connection with the exhortation to
seek the welfare of Babylon, and thus again in the context of
polemic against the false prophets. Finally, it reappears in
30:24 in a way which pointedly alludes to its introduction in
23:20.

The method of the allusion is an almost verbal reproduction

in 30:23–24 of 23:19–20. That passage speaks of the wrath of YHWH having gone forth so as to fall unavoidably on 'the wicked'; moreover, it 'will not turn back until he has executed and accomplished the intents of his mind'. The oracle concludes with the enigmatic phrase: 'In the latter days you will understand this.' In its first context, in *Jeremiah* 23, these words of Jeremiah carry little immediate comfort, except somewhat backhandedly in their implication that YHWH's anger will eventually spend itself and that there will be a time for understanding his purpose in retrospect. In the meantime the activity of the false prophets served only to draw a veil over that purpose and hasten the punishment. In the oracle's new context, however, the force of it is quite different. The allusion to *Jeremiah* 23 has the effect of saying that that purpose of YHWH which was formerly mysterious is hereby made known. The passage is now flanked by others which reaffirm the nation's covenant status. The typical covenant formula ('And you shall be my people, and I will be your God', *cf.* Ex. 6:7; Lv. 26:12) precedes it (22). And the verse that follows it echoes the time reference in the words 'In the latter days' with the phrase 'At that time ...' (31:1), which in turn introduces the chapter that contains the promise of the new covenant (31:31–34). It is the renewed promise, coming to its climax in the theology of new covenant, and written in a book by the prophet who *did* know the mind of YHWH (30:1), that constitutes the plans of his mind.

We come now to the method of the argument in the 'Book of Consolation'. The section is not homogeneous, as is evident from a cursory reading. Chapters 30 and 31 are distinguished from 32 and 33 in a way analogous to that which distinguishes the oracular material of *Jeremiah* in general from its more sustained prose-like argumentation. (Similarly, Jeremiah himself is in the background in 30 and 31 but to the fore in 32 and 33.)[18]

As far as 30 – 31 are concerned the treatment of its subject is not in terms of systematic argument. Rather, it proceeds by contrast with familiar motifs in the prophecy. A number of

specific verbal parallels may be observed: terror, 30:5, *cf.*
6:25; pain of labour, 30:6, *cf.* 4:31; 6:24; salvation out of
distress, 30:7, *cf.* 2:27; incurable hurt/wound, 30:12, 15, *cf.*
15:18 (and hurt/wound, in other metaphors, frequently, *e.g.*
4:20; 6:14; 8:21); lovers, 30:14, *cf.* 22:20, 22 (23:23–24);
service/slavery, 30:8–10, *cf.* 2:20; wilderness, 31:2, *cf.* 2:2;
building and planting, 31:4–5, *cf.* 1:10; north-country, 31:8,
cf. 4:6; 3:18; created order, 31:27, 35–37, *cf.* 4:23–26.

The allusions thus recorded are not all of exactly the same
type. Some of them make direct contrasts with the earlier
statements. For example, YHWH's declaration that 'Jacob'
will be saved (30:7b) is in glad antithesis to his condemnation
of the cringing 'Arise and save us!' of 2:27. Of other passages
mentioned above, similar straight reversals occur at 30:8–10;
31:4, 8, 27, 35–37. In other cases the evocation of motifs is
analogous rather to the repetition of the oracle concerning
YHWH's plans, 30:23–24. That is, the contrast with the old
message is effected by providing a new context. Examples are
30:5–7 and 12–17.

The kind of contrast produced by these two passages is of
great significance for the thought-pattern of the 'Book of
Consolation'. It consists, quite simply, in logical *non sequitur*.
30:7bβ illustrates the point. Verses 5–7bα could have constituted one of those oracles which were common in the
earliest chapters of *Jeremiah*, a message of doom. Here, however, it is completed, quite unexpectedly, with the little
phrase: *ûmimmennâ yiwwāšēaʿ* ('and he shall be saved out of it').
It is not even joined to the preceding phrase by a definite
adversative conjunction, but by the simple copula (and). The
word 'yet' (RSV) has to be provided to produce a suitable
sense-flow in English. Salvation does not follow from what the
body of the oracle prepares the hearer for; yet that is what will
come.

The illogicality of YHWH's plans for his people is
expressed even more strongly in verses 12–17. Once again an
oracle is paraded, verses 12–15, which promises only woe. It
has at its heart the incurability of the people's hurt, a motif
which occurs in three of the four verses, *viz.* 12, 13, 15. What

94

follows in verses 16–17 could not be expected. The enemy which was implacable is suddenly overthrown; and YHWH himself will heal the incurable wound. What is most striking, however, is the way in which the two parts of the passage are joined, for verse 16 opens with the conjunction *lākēn* ('Therefore', RSV). Once again the thought-flow is illogical, and the *non sequitur* is highlighted by the conjunction *lākēn*, suggesting causal connection, even more than the unobtrusive copula of verse 7. YHWH will act for Judah, it seems, precisely because of her incapacity to escape from the consequences of her guilt.

The change of gear which happens at verse 17 is maintained, moreover, in the verses that follow. The motif of healing (17) leads naturally into a repetition of the promise to restore 'Jacob's' fortunes (18), and the allusion to Zion in the pathetic phrase 'It is Zion, for whom no one cares!' (17) seems to invite the rejoinder 'the city shall be rebuilt upon its mound, and the palace shall stand where it used to be' (18). Thenceforth the images of salvation continue to the end of the chapter, until the motif of YHWH's plans and *time* connect the thought with chapter 31. The illogicality of YHWH's plan of salvation is sustained, therefore, throughout chapter 30, and opens on to 31.

On the wider plan of biblical covenantal theology there is nothing unusual about this. The theology of illogical grace is present at the close of the flood-narrative (Gn. 8:21),[19] and also in the story of the covenantal renewal after the great apostasy of Sinai (Ex. 34:9).[20] The same theology now reappears in the new covenant. It is, of course, developed in an individual way in *Jeremiah*. Indeed, the element of *non sequitur* is itself a reversal of what had appeared to be *non sequitur* in Jeremiah's unfolding accusation of Judah. The sequence 10:12–16, 17–18 begins with a hymn on the subject of Israel's election, whose euphoric climax (16) is suddenly dashed by an oracle announcing that YHWH 'is slinging out the inhabitants of the land' (17–18). If Israel's election gives way to rejection, then by the logic of new covenant, her reduction in helpless sin and punishment can herald salvation.

95

An atmosphere of renewed permanence suffuses *Jeremiah* 30 and continues throughout the 'Book of Consolation'. The restoration of Zion (18, *cf.* 31:38–40), together with its 'prince' (*'addîr*), verse 21, and even David, verse 9, is in stark contrast with the basic threat which Jeremiah's ministry had posed to the city and the nation's institutions (*e.g.* 7:1–15; 22:30). Every reassurance helps create this atmosphere, sometimes echoing the theology of salvation in Isaiah 40 – 55 (30:10–11; 31:2–14). The note of permanence rises to an insistent strain which appeals to the fixed order in creation itself in order to affirm the fixity of YHWH's purpose to redeem Israel, king, priests and all, irrevocably (31:35–37; 33:14–26).

This triumphant strain, however, raises an obvious theological problem. Much of Jeremiah's early preaching was directed precisely against the conception that Israel's institutions carried a guarantee of permanence. There is, therefore, a massive shift from that preaching to the affirmation of the traditional promises and institutions which is found here. The transformation of Jeremiah from prophet of judgment to herald of salvation, accounted for in the story of the confrontation with Hananiah, has been complete and dramatic! The *volte-face*, however, does not come out of the blue; rather, the tension that the change occasions is part of the theologizing of these chapters, and their purpose is to provide a theological basis for it.[21]

The tension is evident in 31:15–20. In these verses the grief of Israel is evoked in the emotive image of Rachel weeping for her children. The passage stages an interaction between the people (as Ephraim) bemoaning their loss and YHWH suffering it with them. The identification of YHWH with the pain of the people has been well prepared for through his identification with Jeremiah, who in turn felt the people's grief. The culmination of the piece is YHWH's heartfelt cry in verse 20, in which he expresses his inability to cast off his son Ephraim. Such an outpouring on YHWH's part is not new in prophecy here. Indeed it is a striking reprise of the terms YHWH had used in Hosea 11:8–9 to express his agony at the competing necessities to condemn and to love.

The picture of a new life of Israel with YHWH, therefore, does not merely turn the clock back. All will be restored, indeed, but the prospect is not one which simply ignores the need to create a real, responsive relationship between the two parties to the covenant. Verse 18 makes its own contribution to the point when it pictures Ephraim accepting the past punishment graciously, and expressing his readiness to turn back to YHWH. At the same time Ephraim's plea hints at what must be done to put his turning on a firm footing. His 'bring me back that I may be restored' rests on a play on the verb *šûḇ* which is at the heart of the great solution, and indeed of all theological wrestling with the relationship of divine enabling and human responsibility in adequate human response to God. Put more literally it is 'Cause me to turn that I might turn'. In its brilliant succinctness, the Hebrew phrase expresses an antinomy which the theology of new covenant will endeavour to develop and complete.

Jeremiah 31:31–34

The new covenant passage proper, 31:31–34, has been subjected to widely differing interpretations, from assessments which see it as a high point in the theologizing of the Old Testament,[22] to those which regard it as a tired recrudescence of Deuteronomistic legalism.[23] It will be clear that the understanding of it for which we have been preparing belongs with the former rather than the latter. The theology of *Jeremiah* has distinguished itself from that of DtH precisely in its readiness to take its direction from Deuteronomy 30:3 and 6, which both looked forward to a life of Israel beyond a cataclysmic punishment and located the basis of it in an initiative of YHWH affecting the heart of his people. It is within this pattern that the new covenant finds its explanation. In the same connection it becomes intelligible why the promise that focuses upon the 'heart' in verses 31–34 is juxtaposed with 35–37, 38–40, where first the nationhood of Israel is reaffirmed (36), and then the setting for the fulfilment of the promise is seen to be none other than a rebuilt Jerusalem (38–40).

Regarding its context in *Jeremiah*, 31:31–34 both provides an initial climax within the 'Book of Consolation' and takes its cue from expectations aroused earlier, especially in 24:7. In that place YHWH promised: 'I will give them a heart to know that I am the LORD.' And in 30–31 up to this point we have observed a case building for an intervention of YHWH's on the grounds of Israel's inability to obey him. When the 'newness' of the new covenant is boiled down, this is what it comes to: not that it is made with 'the house of Israel and the house of Judah' (31), nor that it is based on *tôrâ* (33), but that *tôrâ* is henceforth to be written on the hearts of the people, in such a way that there will be no further need of teachers in Israel (33–34). The promise of forgiveness of sins (34) is sometimes seen as the essentially new thing in the new covenant, but the argument depends on a low evaluation of other texts. The forgiveness promised here is not introduced as a new concept; rather it comes in the wake of the new possibilities which YHWH is creating by transforming the people themselves.

Jeremiah 32–33

Chapter 32 brings a change of scene and tone, but not of interest. It consists of first- and third-person narratives about Jeremiah, beginning (1–5) with the first recorded direct confrontation of the prophet with King Zedekiah. In focusing on that king the narrative reverts to the theme of the inevitability of the coming disaster, and the impossibility of salvation by resistance to Babylon. It is a set piece which recurs with slight variation at 34:1–5. In the present context (32:3–5), it does not actually record a word of Jeremiah, but rather Zedekiah's question why Jeremiah prophesies of the inevitable fall of both king and city. The words here are Zedekiah's, therefore. This may prompt the question whether they accurately reflect what Jeremiah is saying. The irony more probably consists, however, in the fact that he has evidently heard them very well. This king, alone of kings in the book, actually seeks out the word of YHWH (37:3, 17; 38:14); he simply lacks the will or conviction to respond rightly to it.

If Zedekiah hears but does not hear, it is appropriate that he should receive no direct answer to his question, except insofar as the narrative that follows is conceived as that answer. In it, Jeremiah is instructed to buy a field from his cousin (possibly as 'kinsman-redeemer'; *cf.* Boaz in Ruth 4), as a sign that 'Houses and fields and vineyards shall again be bought in this land' (15). The juxtaposition is not accidental, but produces that same sort of perplexing *non sequitur* which we observed in chapters 30 – 31, a perplexity now apparently felt by the prophet (25). The bulk of the chapter is a meditation on the logic of this latest command to Jeremiah.

The meditation unfolds in two parallel speeches, the prayer of Jeremiah, verses 16–25, and the response of YHWH, verses 27–44. Prayer and response share a premiss which will turn out to be central to the theology both of the 'Book of Consolation' and of the whole prophecy. In verse 17, Jeremiah prays: 'Nothing is too hard for thee ...' and finds an echo in YHWH's rhetorical answer, '... is anything too hard for me?' The prayer and its answer appeal to YHWH's lordship both in creation and in his dealings with the covenant people. Jeremiah's prayer then proceeds to record YHWH's ancient salvation of Israel from Egypt, his gift of the land of Canaan, and Israel's chronic departure from the covenant he had made with them. The logic of the prayer is that the imminent end of the city is the only just outcome of the history he has rehearsed. YHWH's power manifests itself properly against a rebellious people – and thus the command to buy a field in his home territory of Anathoth, though he has done it without demur, makes no sense in the prophet's mind.

YHWH's answer agrees almost completely with Jeremiah's understanding of Judah's condition. He repeats the accusation of the historic nation in terms familiar from earlier parts of the prophecy, calling to mind the abysmal failure of their leaders. He laments their persistence in idolatrous worship, and once again stresses the inevitability of the coming judgment, just as Jeremiah has recently reiterated it for the benefit of Zedekiah. Only in the outcome of the story does YHWH diverge from Jeremiah's account, and then dramatically.

The change comes in verse 36 with another unexpected and illogical *lākēn* ('therefore'; cf. 30:16). What is the consequence of all this chronic sin? The *immediate* outcome, miserable exile in a far land, is put into a perspective which diminishes it in ultimate importance. YHWH deliberately distances himself, verse 36, from the idea that destruction and exile are the definitive destiny of Israel. He raises that spectre here only to attribute it to Jeremiah! (Note the words 'which *you* say' [my italics]; the address is in the plural, possibly drawing in Baruch, or just evoking the general despair in Jerusalem.) He himself forges a wholly different chain of cause and effect, in which the sin of the nation has as its ultimate consequence a regathering from the countries to which he has driven them, and their reconstitution as his people (37–38).

Here, as in chapter 31, the bold *non sequitur* requires a theological grounding. This follows in verses 39–41. It is essentially the same as the new-covenant thinking in 31:31–34, though the term 'new covenant' itself does not appear. The passage consists of a series of statements of intent on YHWH's part, central to which is the twice-repeated declaration that he will give the people a heart to fear him, verses 39–40b. It is the firmest statement, even in the 'Book of Consolation', of YHWH's intention to take matters into his own hands in solving the problem of his people's incapacity to meet the covenantal conditions placed upon them.

The chapter finishes (42–44) by reverting to the matter which sparked the debate, namely the purchase of the field by Jeremiah. YHWH can now affirm with a new credibility that that flamboyant demonstration of a future for Judah really has a basis, despite the doubts in the minds of those who hear his words (43b). This short passage, and the chapter, conclude by repeating the formula borrowed from Deuteronomy 30:3, and now characteristic of the 'Book of Consolation': 'I will restore their fortunes, says the LORD' (44). The conclusion of the whole debate is the answer to the question posed initially by Zedekiah. Jeremiah prophesies the imminent doom of the city (and therefore nation) and dynasty in order that they might ultimately be saved!

Jeremiah 33 adds little substantively new to the picture that 30 – 32 have already painted. It presents the salvation of YHWH as a mystery now revealed (3); it distances YHWH's understanding that there is a future from the natural scepticism of the hearers (10); it contains motifs of health and healing (6), and of desolation redeemed (10–11) which have become familiar. Furthermore, it has its own case of the divine 'illogic' of salvation, where verses 6–9, with their burden of promise focused on the refrain of the 'restoration of fortunes' (7), follow in surprising sequence (though it should no longer surprise) on words presaging immediate judgment at Chaldean hands (1–5). The 'restoration of fortunes' motif recurs at verse 11, and finally closes the 'Book of Consolation' itself at 33:26.

The difference between the present chapter and the preceding, therefore, is hardly in substance, but rather in tone. The restoration of Zion, king and priest, has been adumbrated, it is true, in 30:9, 18, 21; 31:14. But there is a new, explicit insistence here, which calls on the fixity of the created order (with its general background in the unconditional promises to Noah following the flood, Gn. 8:21–22; 9:8–17) to illustrate the irrefragability of the covenant which will now be made.

It is that insistent tone of the chapter which makes it the most intractably difficult to square with the early preaching of Jeremiah. How can the prophet who risked life, reputation and everything to cry to Judah that what seemed fixed and enduring was not so, now perpetrate the very message which he had opposed in others? The question is of the essence of an understanding of the book. It is not significantly less sharp, however, if we follow LXX instead of MT and omit 33:14–26, since the substance of those verses is already implied in the theology of 30–32 as we have expounded it, and not least in the immediate context of the new covenant promise at 31:35–37.[24]

Our argument so far, however, has attempted to provide a context for an understanding of this sharp antithesis between the kind of preaching which has come to be considered typical of Jeremiah (as in 7:1–15) and these unqualified reassurances about the future. Certainly, if one simply compares *Jeremiah* 33 with 7:1–15, without thought for the logical flow of the book in the interim, the verdict can be only that the two are thoroughly incompatible. We have argued, however, that since the confrontation with Hananiah in chapter 28, the reader has been prepared for the transformation of Jeremiah into a salvation-prophet. This has precisely *not* been done so as to equate Jeremiah with his opponents. Rather, it is in the context of a wholly new thing which YHWH intends to do with his people, so that the ancient promises may at last attain fulfilment in a way which deals permanently with Israel's chronic record of failure in respect of her covenant obligations. The theology of the 'Book of Consolation' thus makes its own contribution to the ancient tension built into the covenant itself arising from the need for obedience on the part of a people that could not obey. *Jeremiah* is not the first or only book of the Old Testament to have attempted this; the question was addressed in its own way in Deuteronomy.[25] Nor is *Jeremiah*'s answer hopelessly utopian or idyllic.[26] The question arises, of course, how a *new* covenant can hope to have better success than the old. The 'Book of Consolation' does not offer its answer to this problem in and of itself, but in the context of the book as a whole. The point will be illustrated by the narratives that follow (34–36; 37–39), where the people's hardness of heart will again be in centre stage. Those narratives, as we shall argue, continue the meditation on the theme of the relationship between the divine and the human will in God's purpose of redemption.

Conclusions on the 'Book of Consolation'

We began the present chapter by saying that the characterization of *Jeremiah* as Deuteronomic was obscuring rather than
illuminating. The 'Book of Consolation' illustrates the point.
It is in important respects like Deuteronomy 30:1–6, but not
like DtH (*cf.* 1 Ki. 8:46–53). The question, furthermore,
whether the theology of the new covenant is fresh or banal
can be answered only with an understanding of the whole
tendency of the book. When that tendency is fully examined,
we shall see that the new covenant is part of a complex
answer to the theological problem posed by the exile – a
Jeremianic answer.

As noted earlier, chapters 34 – 36 could be considered
either with the present section or with the following (37 –
44). We shall consider them now.

Jeremiah 34 – 36

The book of *Jeremiah* comes to a people that does not yet
experience the great things promised in the 'Book of Consolation'. It therefore addresses a situation in which the
immediate realities of the exilic, or early post-exilic, period
are still much felt, in which, indeed, the message of *Jeremiah*
may yet have to win its way against rival programmes akin to
those of Hananiah. Even throughout the 'Book of Consolation', the narrative never lost sight of the inevitability and
necessity of subjugation to Babylon. Its horizon now returns
to that message, and will remain there till chapter 45, after
which the oracles against the nations will again pick up the
theme of Judah's salvation and Babylon's demise.

Chapters 34 – 36 do have a certain thematic coherence of
their own, apart from those which, as noted above, chapter
36 shares with chapter 26.[27] Important in them is the focus
once more on Judah's inability to repent effectively, under
the influence of the Davidic kings. The narrative again dis-
cards chronology, proceeding from Zedekiah in 34 back to

Jehoiakim in 36. In fact the shadow of the whole period of Jeremiah's ministry hangs over these chapters because of the implicit presence in them of the figure of Josiah. This is most obvious in the repeated characterization of Jehoiakim as the son of Josiah (35:1; 36:1, 9). But Josiah is subtly present in other ways too, as will appear, and not only the king himself, but the theological thinking surrounding his reign in 2 Kings 22 – 23.

Jeremiah 34 begins with what is virtually a reprise of the confrontation between Jeremiah and Zedekiah in 32:1–5. The repetition is an effective way of bringing the focus back from the dizzying vistas of a glorious future to the actuality of siege and imminent captivity. This time the words are actually Jeremiah's, rather than those which the king attributes to him. Now that the prophet himself speaks, the news appears slightly better for Zedekiah, for though the sentence on him is not revoked, it is tempered by the promise that he will die 'in peace'. The prospect of a decent funeral, verse 5, is also no negligible thing, and is in fact one of those turns for the better which occur between the former and latter parts of the book (contrast 16:6–7).

There are, however, disturbing undertones. First, the promise that Zedekiah will die 'in peace' is overshadowed by what happened to Josiah when he was assured that he would be 'gathered to his grave in peace' (2 Ki. 22:20). The difference in the precise terminology hardly diminishes the force of the parallel (especially as verse 5 directs attention specifically to Zedekiah's funeral, which was also the focus in the case of Josiah). The 'peaceful' funeral of the former king was, of course, an ambivalent blessing in the end, because it was the consequence of a premature and violent death.[28] The analogy itself, therefore, renders the promise to Zedekiah somewhat ambivalent.

Secondly, however, this ambivalence is in the nature of the case. The force of the promise to Zedekiah is inevitably mitigated by the repeated declarations of Jeremiah that he could not avoid the coming Babylonian invasion, with all the attendant miseries of defeat and captivity. This 'peace' is pale from the outset. And in the event, Zedekiah does not avoid the horror of seeing the death of his sons and his own mutilation (39:6–7; 52:10–11), before he is dragged off to dismal life-imprisonment. The prophecy of death in 'peace' has more than a tinge of irony, therefore. It may reflect on the torment to which the king was subject while he maintained his fragile hold on the doomed kingdom, inadequate to the conflicting pressures from prophet on the one hand and princes on the other (*cf.* 38:14–28), but presiding in the end over the *šeqer* of which Jeremiah had always accused his compatriots, and which was the very antithesis of *šālôm*. Interpreted thus as a piece of irony, the word to Zedekiah in this place is hardly at odds with others in which Jeremiah speaks to him more directly of his coming doom (37:17; 38:17–18).

As significant as the differences between the actual prophecies to Zedekiah are the pericopes which they respectively introduce. 34:6–7 picture the desperate situation of Jerusalem with new force by mentioning that only Lachish and Azeka remain of the fortified cities of Judah. The military vulnerability of Judah is yet another comment on the precipitous fall of the once mighty Davidic monarchy. The account that follows continues the theme. It is a revealing story of Zedekiah's indecisive flirtation with covenant-keeping. For once the king prevailed, if temporarily, over the vested interests of the powerful in Judah, and persuaded them to release their Hebrew slaves, in obedience to the command of Deuteronomy 15:12–18 (Ex. 21:2–6).

The attempt succeeds, however, in revealing only the ineffectuality of the king's best intentions. The people, for no other reason, apparently than their sheer inner resistance to the move, 'turned back' (*wayyāšûbû*) and took their slaves again (*wayyāšîbû*, 11). The incident becomes, in a word of YHWH through Jeremiah, a paradigm of the ancient moral character of the people. In his condemnation of their infidelity over the slaves he takes up the play on *šûb* in the narrative of the incident, and castigates their momentary turning to him which had issued only in a turning away again

(15–16; *cf.* the similar double potential of the verb *šûḇ* in Je. 3:12–14; see above, chapter 1). The incident is finally turned against the people with considerable ironic effect; as they have refused liberty to their slaves, so YHWH proclaims liberty to them, liberty to the sword, pestilence and famine (17)! The pericope then returns to a reaffirmation of the inevitability of the Babylonian captivity. As it does so there is a final crunching use of *šûḇ* (hiph.), verse 22, in correspondence with the people's 'taking back' of their slaves, but now announcing YHWH's 'bringing back' of the forces of the enemy. Covenant breach could not more plainly bring its own punishment in train. (*Cf.* the logic of Jeremiah's early preaching, which had insisted that Judah was bringing disaster upon herself; 2:17–19.)

Zedekiah is solidly at the centre of the whole incident. It was he who initiated the reform, and its failure is a comment on his inability to maintain the Mosaic covenant. More profoundly, it is a comment on the inability of the whole Davidic dynasty to do so. The extrapolation is fair because of the implicit analogy with Josiah's reform. According to our understanding of the account of that reform, its purpose was to show the inescapable failure of the dynasty, even in the face of the best contrary indications. Here, there are few good indications at all. *Jeremiah*, concentrating on Josiah's successors, has never pretended to repose any hope in them. Nevertheless, the analogy with Josiah, already suggested by the comparable prophecy regarding a death 'in peace', can be maintained. Like him, Zedekiah attempts a kind of reform, and in this case too, its only issue is to make embarrassingly clear yet again that dynasty and nation must fall.

With chapter 35 the scene shifts back to Jehoiakim, 'the son of Josiah, king of Judah' (1). Both the lack of interest in chronology and the connection of Jehoiakim back to Josiah suggest that here too the focus is on the potential of the dynasty as such. The connection with Jehoiakim himself is less direct than it was with Zedekiah in the previous episode. Jeremiah's words, when they come, are addressed to 'the men of Judah and the inhabitants of Jerusalem' (13). The prophecy bears on the dynasty, however, first because of the allusion to the king in verse 1, but more particularly because of the analogy between the 'house of the Rechabites' (2) and the Davidic house. This analogy is implicit throughout, but finally laid bare in verse 19, with the phrase 'Jonadab the son of Rechab shall never lack a man to stand before me', so redolent of the dynastic promise (1 Ki. 2:4; 8:25) as reformulated in *Jeremiah* 33:17.

The present chapter contains the fullest characterization in the Old Testament of the eccentric group which here serves Jeremiah's preaching. (Rechab himself is included in the Chronicler's genealogies at 1 Ch. 2:55; for Jonadab, *cf.* 2 Ki. 10:15–17.) On the face of it they are used simply as a paradigm of fidelity, a stick with which to beat the rank and file of Judah (16), and indict the monarchy. In a sense it is not necessary to look further than this. Yet the narrative is not without its ironies. The faithfulness of the Rechabites, in its specific form, is required by no mandate except the decision of its founder. Their 'rule', furthermore, suppresses the very things (6–7) which are held out to Israel for her enjoyment, not only by the terms of the ancient covenant (Dt. 7:13; 8:12–13), but in the firmly agricultural, city-orientated, non-abstemious promises which relate to the time beyond exile (31:12; 32:43–44; 33:10–11) and even in the command respecting their lifestyle in Babylon (29:5). Their very presence in Jerusalem is a measure of their limited capacity even to maintain their principles and lifestyle, compelled as they are to share the straitened circumstances of their more 'orthodox' brethren.

In short, the future held out to the Rechabites is one without the fulness which faithfulness to YHWH (rather than an inventive patriarch) could bring. The Rechabite example operates, in fact, on more than one level. On the one hand it is a straightforward paradigm of fidelity; on the other it compares something that is limited, even negligible, in its capacity to give Judah a future, with something that could be much greater, namely a society more generally faithful to YHWH, with an effective son of David at the helm, and a future full of the good things of the promised land. That greater possibility, however, is conspicuously not realized in Jehoiakim, or any other member of the Davidic dynasty.

A comparison of *Jeremiah* 36 with the story of Josiah's reform (2 Ki. 22 – 23) has been offered at an earlier stage (above, chapter 2). It is necessary only to repeat the conclusions of the argument there. Although *Jeremiah* 36 highlighted contrasts between the two kings' responses to the word, the effects of the two portrayals were similar in the final analysis. As Kings explicitly presented Josiah as a paradigm of faithful rule, so *Jeremiah* 36 does so implicitly, yet neither rests the hope of Judah's future on him. On the contrary, both, in their different ways, show the failure of the monarchy to procure salvation to be quite inescapable. *Jeremiah* 36, therefore, brings the flow of thought since 34:1 to a climax. The issue since then has been the failure of the monarchy, and we have observed implicit allusions to the argument about Josiah in 2 Kings 22 – 23. The analogy with Josiah is most pronounced in *Jeremiah* 36. The complex of narratives in 34 – 36 has the accumulated effect of showing what had also been the theme of DtH, namely the inexorable failure of the Davidic dynasty.

Jehoiakim's attempt to stem the prophetic tide ends, of course, in more failure. The words of Jeremiah are written again, together with 'many similar words' (32). They contain yet another reiteration of the certainty of subjugation to Babylon, including a word for Jehoiakim himself. He may not even hope for the sort of decent burial which would be vouchsafed to Zedekiah; and the sentence 'He shall have none to sit upon the throne of David' (30) carries a last ironic echo of the promise to the Rechabites, which diminishes him even further, as this specifically Jeremianic indictment of the monarchy throws its biggest punch.

Conclusions on *Jeremiah* 34 – 36

The section 26 – 36 ends as it began, therefore, with an indictment of the monarchy. Its latter chapters in particular,

34 – 36, have in common with DtH the belief that the historic
Davidic dynasty was doomed. Jeremiah 36, indeed, echoes
2 Kings 22f., though in doing so adopts a rather different
method of showing the bankruptcy of the monarchy. More
importantly, *Jeremiah* 34 – 36 belongs to a wider argument in
Jeremiah which is decisively different from DtH in looking for
a future, wholly new establishment of the institutions of
Israel, including the Davidic monarchy (23:5–8; 30:9;
33:14–26). The whole section *Jeremiah* 26 – 36 has the 'Book
of Consolation' at its centre. *Jeremiah* 34 – 36 is specifically
linked to the 'Book of Consolation', furthermore, by the
similarity of the words to Zedekiah in 32:1–5. For these
reasons, although *Jeremiah* 34 – 36 agrees with the books of
Kings on the failure of the historic dynasty, its context is in
an argument which offers hope to Judah. That hope is
typical of *Jeremiah*, but not expressed in Kings.

On the other hand, the position of *Jeremiah* 34 – 36 in the
book, following the 'Book of Consolation', places the stubbornness of the human will once again in centre stage. The
chapters thus become part of the continuing reflection on
the relationship between the divine and human wills in the
achievement of salvation. This topic also will be treated in the
section which follows.

CHAPTER FIVE

Choice and destiny (37 – 45)

Jeremiah 37 – 45 have certain general characteristics in common with chapters 25 – 36. A preoccupation with the word of YHWH is at the heart of this part of the book also, as we shall see. And there continues to be reflection on the nature of peace (*šālôm*) and falsehood (*šeqer*). Thus there is more in Jeremiah's exclamation when he is arrested on leaving the city (37:14) than the protest that he is the victim of an isolated falsehood. His cry of '*šeqer*' inevitably reverberates with the whole theme of falsehood in the prophecy hitherto, and says in effect that the attitude of all those about him is and always has been profoundly misguided. This victimization of YHWH's prophet is merely the latest evidence of a nation that resists his word. In contrast, the *šālôm* motif is taken up with some irony in 38:4. Like the salvation-prophets who are their spiritual kin, the princes simply fail to perceive that the way of *šālôm* is through Jeremiah's preaching.

Despite these similarities, *Jeremiah* 37 – 45 unmistakably form a distinct section of the book. There are, in the first instance, formal differences from chapters 25 – 36, of which the most obvious is their adherence to a chronological pattern, and their focusing on the last days of Judah and the immediate aftermath of its fall. The figure of the prophet is never far from the foreground.

If our section has new features by comparison with 25 – 36, it nevertheless has strong links with the chapters that immediately precede that section, especially 21:1–10; 24, and the perspective which came to expression there. Those links are forged, first, by certain superficial similarities. The sending of Pashhur the son of Malchiah and Zephaniah the priest to Jeremiah, 21:1, is echoed in 37:3 and 38:1. The separation of these two figures here, and their association with others, suggest that the circumstances are now recorded in a more detailed way than in chapter 21; the latter may therefore be regarded as a relatively schematized rendering of the embassies of Zedekiah to the prophet. More significantly, the phrase 'he ... shall have his life as a prize of war' (21:9) recurs three times in these chapters (38:2; 39:18; 45:5), becoming a kind of leitmotif.

Echoes of this sort, however, merely point to deeper connections between chapters 21 – 24 and 37 – 45. In claiming this, we take issue with G. Wanke, who has made a detailed study of the third-person narratives of the book. Wanke discusses 37–44 in direct relation to 19:1 – 20:6; 26 – 29; 36, but excludes chapter 24, and the 'Book of Consolation', from his consideration.[1] This results, I think, from too heavy an emphasis on the topic of the prophetic role in his study, to the exclusion of other theological topics. We shall return in due course to that topic. In my view, however, the present section is essentially an application of the theology of chapters 21 and 24 to the events that lead up to and into the exile.[2] We shall therefore examine it first of all in that light.

The comparison between the two sections (21 and 24; 37 – 45) can be put in the context of the structure of the whole book. As we have presented that structure, the earlier section brings to a close that first half of the book whose theme was the closing down of hope for Judah. It announced what had been becoming ever plainer, namely that there must be an exile, and added that only so could there be a future for Judah. The people's acceptance of the Babylonian conquest, understood as an instrument of YHWH, became the condition of their enjoyment of the salvation which would come in its wake. Equally, the present section is an affirmation of the same theological perspective following the 'Book of Consolation', which had elaborated the premiss that there was indeed a future beyond the judgment. *Jeremiah* 37 – 45, therefore, relate to earlier material in a complex way. First, the

112

section confirms the rightness of the perspective in chapter 24, by showing that the people as a whole, then the Palestinian remnant in particular, choose their own fates. Second, it continues the theme, made prominent by the 'Book of Consolation', of the relationship between the human and divine wills in relation to judgment and salvation. These two strains, as is evident, belong together in an integrated way.[3]

Jeremiah 37 – 45 may be subdivided into the following sections: 37 – 39; 40:1 – 43:7; 43:8 – 44:30; 45.[4] The first three of these form the main part of the picture that is built up here. They have features in common, and indeed there is a certain parallelism in their unfolding arguments.[5] Each addresses a different scene: Judah in its last days under Zedekiah, up to and including its fall to Nebuchadrezzar (37 – 39); Judah after the same event, under Babylonian rule and tutelage (40:1 – 43:7); the fugitive Jewish remnant in Egypt (43:8 – 44:30). In each case the same message, based on *Jeremiah* 24, comes afresh, together with the response to it.

Jeremiah 37 – 39

The first scene, then, revolves around confrontations between Jeremiah and Zedekiah. These are not in themselves new. As well as the 'arm's length' exchange recorded in 21:1–10, we have now had that of 32:1–5 (which was in fact a quotation of the prophet's words by the king) and 34:1–5, the first actual recorded encounter between the two. The burden of all these exchanges has been substantially similar: judgment is determined against nation, city and king. The softening of the line in 34:4–5, which was in any case not free from irony, did not affect the message materially. The present passage adds two interviews between king and prophet. In the first (37:17) the message is reiterated curtly and without compromise. The second, however, which turns out to be the last, contains a surprise, for in it Jeremiah

113

actually sets before the king a choice which has not been given hitherto: 'If you will surrender to the princes of the king of Babylon, then your life shall be spared, and this city shall not be burned with fire, and you and your house shall live' (38:17).

Discussions of the different words of Jeremiah to Zedekiah have often seen the variations within them as betraying the conflicting theological interests of different redactional hands.[6] This approach misses a dimension of the narrative, however. It may not be accidental that the confrontation which appears to give Zedekiah an actual chance to repent is the last one recorded, in the very teeth of the fulfilment of the words directed against him. The paradoxical effect of the 'last offer', as it were, with its surface implication that the king's demise is not after all inevitable, is to seal its inevitability. It does so by revealing the real resistance of Zedekiah to the word. Put another way, it is not that Zedekiah is the helpless victim of an arbitrary word; rather, the prophecies hitherto are shown to be true and just. For all his craven toying with the word of YHWH (37:17), he will never hear it. The final encounter of this king with the prophet results, despite his greater regard for the man than was shown by Jehoiakim, in just as sure an attempt to invalidate his word by its suppression in secrecy (38:24–26). Zedekiah's delusion, finally, that it is he who disposes over the life of Jeremiah (24) is neatly and savagely ironical. It pictures a man whose own perspectives are too deeply ingrained for him to allow access to new ones.

Jeremiah 37 – 38 preserve a dimension of the book which has never been far from the surface, namely the inalienable responsibility of the human actor in the drama of salvation. This dimension appears, for example, on the verge of the new covenant passage, at 31:29, in the rejection of the proverb: 'The fathers have eaten sour grapes, and the children's teeth are set on edge.' Here, in immediate proximity to the new covenant passage, is an answer precisely to the protest that each new generation is powerless to avoid the consequences of the sins of its fathers. On the contrary, each

114

generation must face YHWH on its own behalf.[7]

More prominently, however, the preservation of human responsibility is a datum of the new covenant theology itself. If the theology which is introduced in 24:7 and comes to a head in 31:31–34 and 32:39–40 affirms a new initiative by YHWH in the relationship between himself and his people, it does so in a way which keeps alive the reality of human response. The formula of 24:7 has sometimes been regarded as containing an irreconcilable tension between two different kinds of solution to the problem of Judah's sin, namely by means of her repentance or by means of YHWH's act of grace.[8] The new covenant, however, is precisely an attempt to affirm the need for both of these things. (Whether the solution makes sense is a question which is open to philosophy and theology to debate.) And the encounters between Jeremiah and Zedekiah are part of the construction of this theology. The utterances of judgment against Zedekiah are in the main categorical, but judgment comes in the end because he does in fact refuse the word of salvation. There is an analogy with the situation of Judah in relation to the prophecy as a whole. (Note the interesting double meaning in the final phrase of 38:27, literally 'for the matter [dābār] had not been heard', meaning, first, the conversation had not been overheard; but second, perhaps, 'the word (of YHWH) had not been heard'. In this allusive meaning it is a final comment on the reign of Zedekiah.)

The section 37 – 39 finishes with the report, in chapter 39, of the fall of Judah and the exile of the king together with anyone of any significance in Judah. It functions, therefore, to validate Jeremiah's prophecies, in both the wider and immediate contexts. The account requires further treatment only in connection with the role of the prophet in these chapters, which we shall take up below. The important refrain 'you shall have your life as a prize of war' (18) will be discussed in the same connection.

115

Jeremiah 40:1 – 43:7

The second subsection of 37 – 45 is 40:1 – 43:7, which deals with the situation in Judah after the Babylonian armies have gone and only a disadvantaged remnant is left in the ancient land. The passage falls, in turn, into two parts, the first, 40:1 – 41:18, setting the scene for a new confrontation between Jeremiah and the people which is the subject of the second (42:1 – 43:7).

At first glance it seems odd that Jeremiah, given the choice, should decide not to go to Babylon with the exiles (40:1–6). Has he not argued consistently that the only way of salvation for Judah, or any Jew, was through the fires of captivity? The immediate answer to the problem seems to be that he regards the new situation in Judah to be of a piece with the exilic experience. This is Judah under the Babylonian yoke, and when Jeremiah opts to join the Babylonian appointee Gedaliah, he is both submitting to that yoke (as he had always advocated that his countrymen should) and remaining among the people in his capacity as mouthpiece of YHWH.

If Jeremiah appears to believe that the remnant in Judah is undergoing the exilic experience, Gedaliah certainly does so. This is clear from his words to the people in 40:9: they may dwell in the land and 'serve the king of Babylon'. 40:7–12, indeed, depicts a brief respite from the fear and urgency that otherwise pervades these chapters. The news that Nebuchadrezzar has appointed a governor in Judah brings a flood of exiles back to the land from places such as Moab, Ammon and Edom, to which they had fled in earlier (unidentified) straitened times. There is plenty in the land. The picture, indeed, is more than idyllic; it is a foretaste of what Judah might be when the debt of exile is paid on a larger scale, and YHWH brings his people back to their land.

It is also, sadly, short-lived. The community has a duly appointed leadership, but has been left weak. The murder of Gedaliah by Ammonite *agents provocateurs* leads to a popular uprising against the assassins, which, though successful, raises the possibility of Babylonian reprisal for the death of the governor. The Judeans' train of thought is natural enough. But the words 'they ... stayed ... near Bethlehem *intending to go to Egypt*' (41:17) are altogether more ominous in the context of the thought of the book. As in *Jeremiah* 24, and lately in 37 – 39, the issue here is once again the decision between Babylon and Egypt. And though the dilemma has never been crueller than here, the message will be the same.

It is thus that Jeremiah enters the scene again. Like Zedekiah before them, the people, under the new, spontaneous leadership of Johanan ben Kareah and others, ask for a word from YHWH. Jeremiah's message, which comes after some delay (42:7), confirms the view that YHWH's purpose for these, who had missed exile through no doing of their own, was that they should endure the Babylonian yoke in the land. Circumstances, therefore, have occasioned what looks like a change in the message: according to the former vision, remaining in the land could not be contemplated (24:8); now it is categorically required. The vital factor that is shared with 24:8, however, is the command not to return to Egypt. To that end Jeremiah's word to Johanan and the people contains a reassurance that they have nothing to fear from Babylon. The prohibition of a return to Egypt stands.

In adopting the view thus outlined, we take issue with those interpretations which look for the difference between chapters 24 and 42 in conflict between different redactional sources. Pohlmann, for example, has argued that an original layer of chapter 42 entertained hopes for YHWH's dealings with the people in Judah which were independent of his purposes for the exiles in Babylon. The chapter then went through several stages of editing, and was finally (42:22) brought into line with the view expressed in 24, namely that hope for the future existed exclusively through and for the exiles. The condemnation of Johanan and his followers when they choose to go to Egypt is part of that redaction.[9]

Pohlmann's view, however, is strained. The finality of 42:22 derives entirely from the logic of its context, not from conflict with it. It is the upshot of the opportunity that is set before Johanan to hear YHWH's word, an opportunity which is passed up. The train of thought in the encounter between Jeremiah and the leaders in Judah following Gedaliah's murder is, in fact, analogous to that in the last confrontation between the prophet and Zedekiah. In that place there was a real appeal to the king to abandon his resistance to Babylonian captivity and be saved. His rejection of this final opportunity confirmed and validated the earlier categorical pronouncements of his fate. Similarly, in the present context, there is once more a real offer to the remnant in Judah, which is nevertheless likewise rejected. And once again, therefore, what had been presented as something absolutely determined in *Jeremiah* 24 is effected by the actual decision of those involved.

The decision, of course, has been catalysed by the mischievous intervention of Ammon, without which, in all likelihood, the remnant in Judah would have considered the threat from Babylon to be past, and lived contentedly in the newly abundant homeland. The murder of Gedaliah, however, has the effect of forcing them to make their own response to YHWH's word. Simply to accept the consequences of the invasion, which had turned out favourably for them, would have said nothing about their response to YHWH in the matter. The condition upon which residence in the land might count as endurance of the Babylonian yoke was their acceptance of YHWH's word that they would be safe from Babylonian reprisal. Gedaliah's murder, therefore, creates a situation partly analogous to that which had preceded Nebuchadrezzar's final visit. It requires the remnant's acceptance *on their own behalf* of his purposes for them by the instrumentality of Babylon, which YHWH had repeatedly made clear through the preaching of Jeremiah.

The interpretation thus offered may be put in the light of 24:8. There, the catalogue of those who are considered 'bad figs' includes 'those who remain in the land, and those who dwell in the land of Egypt'. The story of the remnant in Judah in our chapters confirms the moral identity of the two groups. Indeed it establishes their *actual* identity, for it is 'all the people' (43:4) who join Johanan and the commanders in disobeying the command to stay in the land, and 'all the remnant of Judah' (43:5), including those who have previously returned from other places of exile, who now migrate together to the land of a more ancient captivity. The outcome of the drama after the fall of Jerusalem was never in doubt; the notice in 41:17 ('intending to go to Egypt') had already warned that there would be no other outcome than that which is recorded. The effect of the present section in its entirety, therefore, is to confirm the identification asserted in 24:8 of those who would stay in the land and those who would look finally to Egypt.

Jeremiah 43:8 – 44:30

Given the theological judgments which have already been passed on the taking of refuge in Egypt, it is perhaps surprising that there is a sequel to the preceding scene which is played out in that land. Yet this final episode in the narrative of events after the fall of Jerusalem has an internal development which in its turn resembles its two predecessors. It is framed by prophecies against Egypt (43:8–13; 44:30). The former has a function similar to the hint that was dropped in 41:17 that the people in Judah would inexorably set their faces to go to Egypt. It announces that, on one level, there is an issue that is settled beforehand. The latter oracle establishes again that those who have gone to Egypt are on a par with Zedekiah in his resistance to YHWH's purpose through Babylon.

Between these two oracles, however, there is an actual encounter between the people and the word of YHWH. Here as in the preceding scenes, therefore, the underlying judgment, stemming from 24:8 and repeated in the frame of the section, is put up for validation in the events that are played out. The tone of the challenge that is set before the remnant in Egypt is, in the nature of the case, rather new. The choice can no longer be between going to Egypt or not.

The accusation by the prophet therefore reverts to a more general critique of the people's idolatrous disposition, in continuity with that of their fathers. The retrospect over past failures has that note of sad resolution to punish, which characterized those parts of the book where the inevitability of judgment became explicit. The reference to 'my servants the prophets', for example, also occurred at 25:4, and has the effect of deliberating on possibilities of repentance now past. The same mood prevailed, incidentally, in 2 Kings 17, where the phrase also occurs (cf. 13–14).

Nevertheless, the word that comes to the Egyptian exiles is contemporary and urgent, as the phrase 'to this day' stresses (10; cf. again 2 Ki. 17:34). YHWH's decision to punish them (11) is immediately based on their persistence in the past sins of Israel (10). The declaration of the people in verse 16: 'As for the word which you have spoken to us in the name of the LORD, we will not listen to you', is crucial. So is the scathing jibe of Jeremiah in verse 25, when he says, echoing their resolve to perform their vows to the queen of heaven: 'Confirm your vows and perform your vows!' The effect of the exchanges between prophet and people, typified in these passages, is to show that, even in Egypt itself, after what had seemed the final doom-laden decision to go there, YHWH still punishes on the grounds of an actual, fresh disposition to reject his word. As in the preceding two episodes, it is only after a new encounter between people and word has been played out that the theme of the inescapable finality of judgment returns.

The picture is not as neat as the foregoing might suggest. The judgment that is uttered leaves room for a few survivors to return in due course to Judah (14, 28), possibly to join in the blessings which have otherwise been held out to those who will return from Babylon. In this respect also, the present chapter has affinities with 2 Kings 17, which had implicitly extended to the contemporary inhabitants of the northern territory the possibility of effectively entering a covenant relationship with YHWH, and had thus become one of the fragile grounds offered by DtH for some future hope (2 Ki. 17:35–40).[10] The finale of the Jeremiah narrative shies away similarly from an irrevocable exclusion even of those who have resolutely cut themselves off from help.

Nevertheless, the overriding tendency of this section, in common with 37 – 45 as a whole, is to confirm the validity of the basic judgment expressed in 24. It takes away some of the sting of the implication that fates are sealed by a divine fiat which leaves no room for the human factor in the making of destinies. As the new covenant theology does not override that factor, but pictures the human and divine wills acting in harmony, so its obverse, the word of judgment against those who will not be party to that covenant, is shown equally to respect that human factor. The judgment comes upon those who, by their own antagonism to the word of YHWH, have willed it for themselves. This match between human will and human destiny was a theme of the prophecy before the new covenant was presented as an answer to chronic inability to obey. The effect of 37 – 45, as indeed of the 'Book of Consolation', is to show that the same basic harmony prevails afterwards. The new covenant does not abolish the human will.

Jeremiah 45

Jeremiah 45 stands somewhat aside from the main argument of the preceding chapters. Nevertheless, as we observed in our remarks about the structure of 25 – 45, it makes connections both with what precedes it and with what follows. The reference to the words which Jeremiah spoke to Baruch in the fourth year of Jehoiakim (1) links the passage unmistakably with chapter 36 (so clearly indeed that it has been thought to have been originally connected with it).[11] In one sense it is an extension to Baruch of the kind of assurance which is typically given to Jeremiah himself, adopting vocabulary both from the Confessions (3, *cf*. 15:10) and from the call-narrative (4, *cf*. 1:10), and thus relates to the theme of the role of the prophet (on which see below). The echoes of the call-narrative, however, also draw the chapter into the

121

mainstream of theological discussion in the book. Significantly, only the negative parts of the planting/plucking up and building/breaking down imagery are affirmed here (4). In this connection the chapter's present position in the book is intelligible. It is at once a suitable sequel to the narrative in chapter 36 (with which it is formally linked), in the sense of reaffirming the sentence pronounced there on the historic dynasty, and to 37 – 44. The phrase which connects most interestingly with those chapters is 'that is, the whole land' (4). Chapters 37 – 44 recorded the fall of Jerusalem, but did not leave the matter there. Rather, they carried the story to a bitter end in rejection of the word of YHWH in Judah even after the fall of Jerusalem (and on into Egypt). The word to Baruch is a sad comment on the thoroughness both of the apostasy and of the consequent judgment. The further threat to 'all flesh' widens the scope of the judgment and prepares for the oracles against the nations.

By virtue of its preparation for the oracles against the nations, however, the word to Baruch should not be taken to represent a theology of unrelieved gloom. We have already noticed that the present chapter has a particular link with the close of the oracles against the nations (51:59–64), because in that place it is Baruch's brother Seraiah who is to deliver Jeremiah's words against Babylon in the city itself.[12] The message to Baruch and the delivery of the words of judgment on Babylon by his brother frame the oracles against the nations. And as we shall see, the oracles against the nations will revive, in their own way, the great hopes expressed by the 'Book of Consolation'. The word of Baruch, therefore, bearing little of hope for Judah in itself, merely puts the story on pause. Furthermore, the shift of interest from Jeremiah, whose story is almost ended, to Baruch, may not owe so much to interest in Baruch for his own sake. Rather, it throws the attention on to the words of Jeremiah, of which Baruch has been the faithful recorder. If Jeremiah must shortly pass from the scene, his words will not. And where the word of God is, there is also hope.

Conclusions

The message of *Jeremiah* 37 – 45 has sometimes been thought to relate only contrastively to other parts of *Jeremiah*. Wanke, for example, thought that each of the units that made up 37 – 45 portrayed in turn the failure and ineffectiveness of the prophet. This was in contrast, therefore, to 19f., 26 – 29, 36, which, though fully recognizing the opposition to the prophet, had regularly *affirmed* him.[13] Kessler too found it hard to reconcile this stark message of doom with the large amount of hopeful material in the book.[14] In contrast with these, our account attempts to relate the message of 37 – 45 not only to the other third-person material in the second half of *Jeremiah*, but also to *Jeremiah* 24 and the 'Book of Consolation'. In doing so, we have taken the view that the theme of these chapters is not merely, nor even primarily, the role of the prophet, which is the assumption of Wanke.[15] Rather, it is a theodicy which justifies God's immediate judgment on Judah in the context of a discussion of the relationship between divine word and human response which is raised by the double sentence passed in *Jeremiah* 24 (whose positive side is developed in turn in the new covenant theology of the 'Book of Consolation'). That is, the condemnation of Zedekiah and his associates is not a divine *fiat* which they could not resist, but a consequence of their determined choice.

The treatment of this issue in *Jeremiah* is one more factor which distinguishes it from DtH. Because DtH has not adopted the solution to the problem of Israel's covenant unfaithfulness which is taken up in *Jeremiah* 24 and the 'Book of Consolation' (namely the new intervention of YHWH enabling the people to obey), it follows that it does not need to raise the issue which we have identified in *Jeremiah* 37 – 45 (that is, the consequent question of the relationship between the divine word and human response). Here, then, is one possible explanation why the present chapters are found in *Jeremiah*, but have no counterpart in DtH (apart from the account of the fall of Judah in 2 Ki. 24:18 – 25:30, which is in

123

any case paralleled in *Jeremiah* 52). The relationship of *Jeremiah* 37 – 45 to Deuteronomy is closer, because of the similarity between Deuteronomy 30:1–6, on the one hand, and *Jeremiah* 24 and the 'Book of Consolation' on the other. *Jeremiah* 24, the 'Book of Consolation' and *Jeremiah* 37 – 45, taken together, may be seen as an extended reflection on the passage in Deuteronomy.

CHAPTER SIX

The figure of Jeremiah (26 – 45)

In our study of *Jeremiah* 37 – 45 we noted that part of the interest there was in the role of the prophet. According to Wanke, indeed, this was the main uniting theme of that section of the book.[1] It is time now, therefore, to focus on it, not for chapters 37 – 45 alone, however, but for the greater part of the second half of the book, chapters 26 – 45.

Jeremiah's cry of despair in 20:14–18 raised the expectation, as we saw, that he would play some further role in the book.[2] That expectation is fulfilled, even on the most superficial of investigations, by the large quantity of material in *Jeremiah* 26 – 45 which relates aspects of the prophet's life and ministry. We began to see, furthermore, something of how the man functions in relation to his message in this part of the book. The Temple sermon as it appears in chapter 26 is not interested in the persecution of Jeremiah in and of itself, but rather in the resistance to the word of YHWH in Judah. The story of Uriah, who appears only here in the prophecy, is told to make the point that it is not the individual prophets who constitute the issue, but only as they stand for the word of YHWH. Similarly, in the conflict between Jeremiah and Hananiah it is above all else an *issue* that is at stake, namely how to discern which prophet really has the word of YHWH.

In these instances the role of Jeremiah is very much as the bearer of the word. This aspect of his persona is developed in relation to the written word. With his letters to the exiles (chapter 29) and also with the two scrolls which he prepares, first for, then in spite of, Jehoiakim, the word moves towards being a thing that has its own existence. Part of this, no

125

doubt, is an affirmation of the authoritativeness of the written word. (See above on chapter 45.)[3] It is a very different picture from that afforded by the first part of the book, where the word was engendered in the fires of the prophet's alienation and self-doubt. The two pictures are not in competition with each other, however. There are presumably, or rather we as readers are expected to make, connections between the utterances in 1–20 and the persecutions which are related in and after 26. Indeed 11:18–23 and 18:18 point to the appropriateness of the assumption. The one picture, therefore, portrays the word of God through the experience of the prophet, in its character as revealer of YHWH; the other sees it as it is perceived and received by the community. The fact corresponds to a shift of interest towards the fate of the community in view of the word of judgment that has been pronounced over it.

The confrontations between Jeremiah and the kings are a special case of the role of the prophet as the speaker of the word. They are much more than arguments between stubborn men. Rather they portray a conflict which is an inescapable part of the constitution of a society. The encounters between prophet and king in the book are in the context, as they must be, of a whole social organization. There are priests and prophets, king and princes, and last but not least, the 'people'. The complex social structure into which the prophetic word comes is well staged in certain of the episodes, not least the Temple-sermon incident (chapter 26) and the reading of the scroll to Jehoiakim (chapter 36). In the former, furthermore, the component parts of the society are portrayed as potentially mobile. Jeremiah is first opposed by an alignment of 'the priests and the prophets and all the people' (7). In verse 11 'the priests and the prophets' find themselves in dialogue with 'the princes and all the people', the people thus entering into a new alignment, though it is not yet clear whether their attitude to Jeremiah has changed. By verse 16, however, the new alignment is defending Jeremiah against the prophet-priest axis, which is now evidently shorn of its popular support.[4] Princes and people still emerge well from chapter 36. During the Babylonian siege, however, even the princes appear to have had enough, and now demand the death penalty for Jeremiah (38:4).

The political issue in *Jeremiah* is often depicted as being a fairly simple one, as between pro- and anti-Babylonian parties in Judah, which furnish the historical background to the real matter, namely loyalty to YHWH. Things are in fact more complex than this, however. The political issue is of the stuff of the argument. At its heart is the question how Judah, in its structures, may be the people of YHWH. Kings, princes, prophets and priests are the cast in a drama whose subject is how human power may be constituted and wielded in a nation that is under the authority of YHWH's word. It is no little part of Judah's failure to be the people of YHWH that her body politic as a whole cannot hear his command. The fickleness of the individual actors is a symptom of a thoroughgoing malaise.

The political milieu of the action is nowhere clearer than in the narrative of the fall of Judah itself, chapter 39. The whole affair is conducted between kings and princes. It is a state machinery, presented as a roll-call of Babylonian dignitaries, that comes to depose the state machinery of Judah, king for king, prince for prince. The subjugation of a people is achieved by the incapacitation of its leaders. It is sufficient, then, simply to take ordinary people captive, and even leave the lowliest behind.

Jeremiah himself, however, merits special attention by Nebuchadrezzar's senior task-force (13–14). The little scene means to say that Jeremiah is a rather important international figure, recognizable by the Babylonian authorities and requiring careful treatment. It could even be said that Jeremiah's depiction in the book is precisely as a king, the king that the representatives of the Davidic dynasty could not be, one who truly operated in the international arena and wielded influence over nations' fates. In any case, the prophet, in his confrontations with kings (and implicitly whole structures), reflects what a properly ordered society under YHWH should be. Nebuchadrezzar's recognition of him, furthermore, is a kind of acknowledgment that he represents a true centre of authority in Judah.

There is a sense too in which Jeremiah's experience symbolizes the condition of the nation. This is true especially in a connection that has the status of motif in 26 – 45, namely imprisonment. Throughout these chapters the prophet's freedom is more or less restricted, and always threatened. If he is not actually in prison his movements are limited, as when in the reign of Jehoiakim he is banned from the Temple precinct (36:5), and he even receives the friendly advice that he and Baruch should go into hiding (36:19). His fortunes evidently fluctuated under Jehoiakim. He enjoyed greater freedom, apparently, at the time of his demonstration with the Rechabites (35:4) and also, of course, when he delivered the Temple sermon (26:1–2). *After* the Temple sermon, however, he is protected from harm only by the tutelage of Ahikam, itself perforce a kind of restriction (26:24).

Jeremiah apparently enjoys spasmodic freedom in Zedekiah's time also. It is in this period, however, that his position in Judah becomes parlous, and he is actually imprisoned. The course of events has to be pieced together from several notices which themselves are not primarily concerned with chronology. His incarceration, however, begins in the 'house of Jonathan' (37:15), during the final Babylonian siege, immediately after he is arrested on the false charge of deserting to the enemy. Subsequently, on appeal to the king, he is transferred to the court of the palace guard and kept in more humane conditions (37:21). Even then there is an attempt to dispose of him in the miry cistern located in the court of the guard, from which he is saved only by the intercession of Ebed-melech with the king (38:4–13).

When we have sketched the chronology of Jeremiah's imprisonment in this way, we are in a position to observe the pattern of allusion to it in the narrative. The first reference comes, out of sequence, at 32:2, and thus helps set the tone for the narrative that follows. (Jeremiah is clearly still at liberty in 34.) The entire episode of the field-purchase, together with the extended exchange with YHWH that follows, is set during Jeremiah's sojourn in the court of the guard, allowing the shades of the prison-house to hang darkly upon all the ensuing narrative in a way which a more faithful chronological rendering could not.

As important as this freedom with chronology in the use of the imprisonment motif is the juxtaposition of its first appearance (32:2) with an allusion to the Babylonian siege. This too is the first such allusion in the narrative, it also coming out of chronological sequence. It seems, therefore, that there is a connection between the imprisonment of Jeremiah and the containment of Judah in besieged Jerusalem, and even that the arrangement of the material is designed to highlight the analogy between the two things as a main motif of the account. The impression is strengthened by the tendency, in what remains of the narrative, for Jeremiah's freedom to become circumscribed *pari passu* with the increasingly straitened position of Judah under the advance of the enemy. Thus, in 34 Jeremiah is still free, and, although the writing is on the wall for Judah, Lachish and Azekah continue to hold out, with Jerusalem, against Babylon (34:6–7). In 37:4–5, we are told that Jeremiah has not yet been put in prison, and then immediately learn of the temporary withdrawal of the Babylonian army because of the approach of the army of Pharaoh. The juxtaposition of the note about the prophet's freedom with news of the respite for Jerusalem is a mirror-image of that which we observed in 32:2.

The turning-point for Jeremiah comes when he is arrested at the moment of exercising his freedom by setting out for Anathoth (37:12 – once again brought into connection with the withdrawal of the besiegers). It now gradually becomes clear that he is to remain in prison until the city falls. The first hint to this effect comes in 37:22, when it is said that he was given a loaf of bread from the street of the bakers daily *until all the bread in the city was gone*. This has the effect both of bringing the fate of Jeremiah into close relationship with that of the city, and of showing that the end for the city is not far off. Then at 38:28 we read simply: 'And Jeremiah remained in the court of the guard until the day that Jerusalem was taken.' The account of its capture ensues without more ado (39).

The motif of Jeremiah's imprisonment meshes, finally, with the criticism through his ministry of the political establishment. The treatment meted out to the prophet in the last days of the kingdom becomes an ironic comment on the position and authority of the king. That is, there is in every decision of Zedekiah's about Jeremiah a reflection on his own fate. This aspect of the meaning of the narrative only appears in 37 – 39, in the teeth, therefore, of the fall of the kingdom. Only at this late state does the question begin to arise of Zedekiah's power to govern the fate and circumstances of the prophet. Thus in 37 it is the princes who imprison Jeremiah without reference to the king. Zedekiah can send for him, and put the prophet's custody on a more humane footing. When the heat is turned back on Jeremiah, however, Zedekiah, almost Pilate-like, has to admit to the princes: 'Behold, he is in your hands; for the king can do nothing against you' (38:5). It is left to Ebed-melech (of the pregnant name: of which 'king' is he servant? YHWH?) to oppose the princes with an effective authority. Against this background Zedekiah's last interview with Jeremiah is pathetic, because of his delusion that he still has some say in the destiny of the prophet (despite his pitiful backward glance at the princes, 25), his incomprehension of the imminence and totality of the disaster, and his failure to see that it is he who is in reality the powerless captive he fancies Jeremiah to be (38:24–28).

'A prize of war'

A final motif that pertains to the fate of the prophet is that which promises to various individuals, and to those in general who submit to the Babylonian yoke, that they shall have their lives 'as a prize of war', 45:5 (*wᵉnātattî lᵉḵā 'eṯ napšᵉḵā lᵉšālāl*). The meaning of the phrase is that those who meet the conditions laid down will escape with their lives. It has been well observed that there is a note of irony about it, the irony of the soldier who remarks wryly that his only 'booty' in some narrow squeak was his life itself.[5]

The phrase is introduced in 21:9, in that first Zedekiah sequence, but otherwise occurs only in 37 – 45 (38: 2; 39:18; 45:5). In its first two occurrences it is addressed to all who have ears to hear, and the strict requirement is to 'go out to the Chaldeans'. (It is not hard to see why Jeremiah was suspected of doing just that at 37:13!) In the two last-named places, however, it is addressed to Ebed-melech and Baruch respectively. In the case of Ebed-melech the condition has modified slightly, and he receives the promise simply because '. . . you have put your trust in me, says the LORD' (39:18). With Baruch the condition is not spelt out (45:5), but may be presumed to be the same as that which obtains for Ebed-melech, in his case a reward for his faithful service of Jeremiah.

Strictly, the promise is not addressed to Jeremiah himself, except in the sense that he is included in the general expression of it (21:9; 38:2), and that he may be presumed to have met the conditions that were also fulfilled by Ebed-melech and Baruch. This is perhaps a sufficient basis, however, to ask whether the promise illuminates in any way the role of the prophet. *Jeremiah* 1 – 20 saw the prophet stand in an analogous position to the whole people; he stood sometimes for Judah just as he stood sometimes for YHWH. The imprisonment motif, furthermore, has suggested a similar fusion of fate of prophet and fate of nation. Is it the case, then, that Jeremiah's escape with his life points somehow to a similar escape for Judah? The question may be redrawn so as to bring in Ebed-melech and Baruch. The nub of the principle established by Jeremiah's standing for the whole people is that a faithful Israelite may do so. The representative status of Jeremiah may even, therefore, be extended in the closing stages of the book to these other true adherents of Yahwism.

The fate of all three is one of the curiosities of the book. Of Ebed-melech nothing more is said after Jeremiah's word of assurance to him (39:16–18). We are no doubt intended to infer that his life was indeed saved, though it is not clear whether he was taken to Babylon or was forced to go to Egypt with Johanan ben Kareah. Of Baruch it is reported that he joined Jeremiah in the trek south (43:6). We are left, however, to guess how their lives progressed, let alone ended, after their arrival in Tahpanhes, apart from the brief glimpse of Jeremiah's preaching there.

This, of course, fits the purpose of the narrative perfectly well. The promise was only that they should escape with their lives, and this they have done, though Jeremiah must have felt more than once that he could not count on it. As regards Jeremiah himself, there is a certain analogy between his situations at the end of 1 – 20 and at the end of the book. In 20 we left him carrying a standard for Judah, at a point in the argument where Judah's fate has been sealed. He, however, has been told that he will be 'restored' (15:19), a promise which is subsequently echoed in respect of the whole nation at 31:18. Jeremiah, it seems, has bridged a gap for Judah/Israel between the judgment and the restoration. In his salvation lay an earnest and symbol of the people's.

It is significant, therefore, that at the end of the book he remains alive. In his life the life of Judah is still epitomized. The exile looks like a kind of death, but the nation is merely dormant, awaiting revival. As much has been spelt out in Jeremiah's own words, of course (29:10–14), but his own survival, and perhaps especially the fact that he has already received his freedom at the behest of a Babylonian pleni-potentiary, is a confirmation of the point. Mere survival, of course, is far less a good than the lyrics of the 'Book of Consolation' had held out to the exiles. For a community that was still in thrall, however, there had to be a descent to the realities of the present tense. And the liberation (from one perspective at least) of the one who must increasingly have been seen to have been the true interpreter of YHWH's will may have spoken hope in itself. Faithful 'Judah' cannot be held by Babylon; the glories promised by the vindicated prophet of YHWH may yet follow.

Conclusions

Reflection on the role of the prophet, so important in *Jeremiah* 1 – 20, continues in the second half of the book. It is a somewhat different kind from that which is found in the earlier chapters, focusing less on the inner life of the prophet, as symbol of the relationship between YHWH and the people, than on his function in the body politic. His role, however, is more interesting than Wanke's characterization of it as representing the rejection of the word of YHWH by Judah and the exiles.

The two main features of that role are the hints afforded by it of the shape of a restored community (by means of the criticism of the structure of the actual one), and the survival of the prophet as an earnest of the survival of the community. It hardly needs to be added that these are interests which arise from *Jeremiah*'s theology of restoration, and which therefore distinguish the book once again from DtH.

CHAPTER SEVEN

The oracles against the nations (46 – 51)

Our treatment will not be complete without some attention to the block of material known as 'the oracles against the nations' (OAN). We have already noticed this section in connection with our discussion of the structure of the book, because of the major difference between LXX and MT in regard to it. (LXX, it will be recalled, located the OAN after 25:13.) The OAN, therefore, raise special problems of their own. This is not only because of the complicated text of *Jeremiah*, however, but also because the OAN are frequently viewed as a phenomenon in their own right within the study of prophecy. It will be beyond our scope to attempt a comprehensive review of the subject, therefore. Rather, we shall be primarily concerned with whether the OAN of *Jeremiah* function within the book in a way that is coherent with the main theme that we have otherwise seen developed there. Some remarks are necessary, however, on the OAN's history of interpretation with respect to *Jeremiah*.

The OAN in the interpretation of *Jeremiah*

There has been a strong tendency in *Jeremiah* studies to regard the OAN as a collection of secondary additions to the book. Duhm (following the classic literary-critical treatment of the subject by Schwally, 1888) saw the OAN as a 'little book of its own', influenced by the OAN of Amos, Ezekiel and Deutero-Isaiah. The original order of the oracles in the book was hard to recover because they differed in LXX and

MT, and because he could not find any historical evidence in favour of the one or the other. On literary-critical grounds, however, he favoured the priority of the order as in the LXX. The OAN, in any case, were essentially a scholastic product, belonging to the many additions he discovered to the authentic book of *Jeremiah*.[1]

Under the influence of form-criticism the study of the Old Testament's OAN was put on a new footing. Enquiries now aimed to discover an original *Sitz im Leben* for them, such as a ritual assertion of YHWH's judgment on Israel's national enemies in the context of a major cultic festival.[2] Such studies drew variously on Ancient Near Eastern phenomena, such as treaties, whose curses evidently had features in common with the threats of the OAN.[3] Some even claimed, on the basis of parallels in ANE prophetic literature, that the OAN may have been the earliest form of Hebrew prophecy.[4]

A consequence for study of the OAN in *Jeremiah* was that a measure of credence was attached again to the authenticity of at least some of them. Rudolph and Weiser, for example, attributed a good deal of chapters 46 – 49 to the prophet. In doing so they assumed that he would have been familiar with the form and the practice of OAN, and also believed that many of the oracles in particular made sense in terms of Judah's historical situation in the latter part of Jeremiah's ministry, focusing especially on the ascendancy of Babylon over the other nations in question, established by the victory over Egypt at Carchemish in 605 BC.[5] The oracles against Babylon itself, however, they regarded as unauthentic and later. The reasons for this will shortly become clear.

The establishment of the likelihood in principle that Jeremiah might well have availed himself of the OAN form, required that criteria be identified for determining authenticity in the case of particular oracles. One has already been noticed, namely historical plausibility. Formal and historical considerations could not suffice in themselves, however, for a satisfactory account of the OAN. Another inescapable factor was the individual use made of the form by the prophet. Thus in the case of Amos, widely acknowledged as the first of the prophets to have used OAN, it has been well recognized that the form in which we have them owes much to Amos' understanding of his particular call and message, and that in turning the OAN finally against Judah and Israel he has done something individual and new.[6] It is clear that *Jeremiah's* use of the OAN is equally individual. The underlying rationale for OAN in the book is the understanding of Jeremiah as 'a prophet to the nations' (1:5; *cf*. 28:8).

The sense in which he is such is not straightforward, but relates to a complex role based on a working out of the relationships between Israel/Judah, Babylon and certain other nations. Prominent in this theologizing is the turning of the tables on Babylon, the original 'foe from the north', which must endure in turn depredations at the hands of a nation 'out of the north' (50:1). This reversal is a feature of the large-scale structure of the book, as is that of the 'lawsuit' motif, which, formerly directed against YHWH's own people (2:9), is now turned against Babylon, to Israel and Judah's benefit (50:34; 51:36f.). At the level of particulars also, many points of contact have been observed between the language and style of *Jeremiah* in general and that of the OAN. Compare, among many possible examples, 4:16 and 50:2f.; 15:16f. and 50:11; 2:6 and 50:12.[7]

Such observations are only the beginning of the enquiry into the way in which prophets used the OAN. They render highly complicated the attempt to study the oracles as a phenomenon in their own right. One approach has been to try to show how the prophets adapted the forms. Hayes, for example, found early usages of the form in a variety of settings, namely holy war, the cult in general, and the covenant festival in particular. He concluded that the OAN should not be evaluated in terms of any single form-critical *Gattung*; rather, the primary motifs in any given use of the form would reflect one institution or another, depending on the user's interests. Thus Amos' usage reflects the cult, and Jeremiah's war.[8] D. L. Christensen, in an extended treatment of the OAN in the Old Testament, thinks of the 'transformation' of the 'war-oracle', from its early political context, in which prophets confronted kings about national policy, to a usage which was ultimately not concerned with contemporary policy, but was essentially eschatological.[9] By these means attempts were made to bring together form-critical insights with the individual usages found in the prophetic books.

Such attempts, however, have not brought unanimity to the study of the OAN in *Jeremiah*. On the one hand, there are those who see the OAN as a distinctive genre, and tend to minimize their real connection with the main body of the book. Thiel, for example, thinks they had their own discrete tradition-history.[10] Carroll too considers the OAN to be 'independent of the contexts in which they now appear'.[11] He goes on to claim that their differences from other important strands in the *Jeremiah* tradition outweigh the similarities, and thinks that the latter derive from essentially secondary attempts to unite the OAN with the rest of the book. On the other hand, both Christensen and Holladay have found reasons to argue for the authenticity of large parts of the OAN, including much of the Babylon material.[12]

The OAN in the book of *Jeremiah*

With this sketchy overview of the OAN in *Jeremiah* interpretation we come now to look more closely at the reasons why the authenticity of the oracles, especially the Babylonian oracles, has been controversial, and how they might be considered an integral part of the book. Objections to the authenticity of chapters 50 – 51 have centred on their relationship with important themes elsewhere in *Jeremiah*. Rudolph, for example, believed that the Jeremiah who had portrayed Babylon as God's scourge upon Judah, who had foretold a seventy-year exile, and who had actually exhorted the exiles to pray for the welfare of the overlord city (the themes of chapters 27 – 29), could not have proclaimed imminent judgment on the same city in the terms, for example, of 51:13, 33. New also, in Rudolph's view, is the picture of Babylon as having overstepped the limits set for it by YHWH; formerly YHWH's instrument, Babylon is now guilty of the hubris that demands his vengeance upon her (50:24, 29, 31f.; 51:12; 28).[13]

Carroll has taken a similar line, emphasizing it by the fact that both blocks of material (27 – 29 and 50 – 51) are dated to the same year (the fourth year of Zedekiah, 594 BC; 27:1; 28:1; 51:59).[14] Rudolph, Carroll and a number of other commentators also discern a corresponding difference between the portrayals of Judah in the OAN and earlier material; while 25:29 makes Judah the first to suffer at Babylon's hands, 49:12 apparently depicts her as innocent.[15] Finally, 50 – 51 are seen as nationalist and triumphalist by contrast with 46 – 49, which contain 'grace notes' for some at least of the nations.[16]

Both Rudolph and Carroll, therefore, have adduced considerations arising from themes in the book as a whole. Rudolph's view proceeds from an expectation of consistency in the historical Jeremiah. Carroll's is more influenced by his belief that the book simply has many strata which we should expect to differ.[17] Neither, in my view, has taken sufficient account of the developing thematic of *Jeremiah* which we have found to explain a number of the features of the book, and which helps in this case also.

To the general point that 50 – 51 offer a completely different picture of Babylon from 27 – 29 it may be replied that the book has prepared us for some such reversal. Two points may be made. First, while the seventy-year exile in Babylon was, of course, a word of judgment to Judah in the first instance, it did imply the question of what would lie then in store for the conqueror – a question which receives first answers in 25:12–14, 26b. Carroll, who makes his 'part one' of *Jeremiah* end at 25:14, thinks nevertheless that the threat to Babylon does not properly belong there, but rather that in verses 12–14 his 'part two' (*viz.* the OAN, 25:15–38; 46 – 51) has influenced the ending of part one.[18] He has thus forced apart the idea of the seventy-year exile and the word of judgment on Babylon. This seems to me to be gratuitous.

Rather, the logic of chapter 25, with its punishment for Judah followed by that of Babylon, is paralleled by what proves to be the logic of the book as a whole, in which 46 – 51 play an important part. Christensen, arguing against just the view of the book here represented by Carroll, in the belief that the events of 597 BC brought about a sea-change in Jeremiah's preaching, saw that the terrible proclamation of a seventy-year exile would have brought with it the need to hold out hope of salvation in the end.[19]

A second point concerns the role of the prophet. The belief that there are two irreconcilable pictures of Babylon in 27 – 29 and 50 – 51 corresponds to a feeling that the portraits of the prophet in the two blocks of material are also at odds. The prophet of woe, it is thought, could not have appeared in the guise of nationalistic salvation-prophet.[20] We have seen, however, that it was precisely the function of Jeremiah's confrontation with Hananiah to transform Jeremiah from judgment-prophet to one who could offer salvation. This transformation depended on the proclamation of a seventy-year exile to distinguish Jeremiah from those prophets who 'healed the wound of my people lightly'. The transition, furthermore, was a necessary prelude to the 'Book of Consolation'.[21] On a broader canvas it also provides a rationale for Jeremiah's new role as herald of Babylon's doom.

Before going further, it is important to consider briefly *Jeremiah* 49:12, which, as we have seen, has generally been thought to fly in the face of a fundamental tenet of *Jeremiah*, namely that Judah thoroughly deserved her punishment at the hands of Babylon. The verse occurs in the oracle against Edom, and is usually taken to mean (with RSV):

> 'If those who did not deserve to drink the cup ('šer 'ên mišpāṭām lištôṯ hakkôs; viz. Judah) must drink it, will you (Edom) go unpunished?'

Since Duhm, the passage has been thought to originate in some late post-exilic Judean polemic against Edom.[22] I suggest, however, an alternative understanding which seems equally possible. It depends on translating the phrase transliterated above not as RSV, but thus (with Keil and Driver):

'those whose right it was not to drink the cup'

The translation of *mišpāṭ* as 'right' refers to the kind of right that derives from the covenant relationship. Such a use of the word occurs at 1 Kings 8:49, where Solomon appeals to YHWH to hear the prayer of his people in exile, and 'maintain their right' (RSV). The thought of 49:12 is not, therefore, that Judah did not deserve punishment, but rather that judgment properly should not have been her fate, because of her covenant relationship with YHWH.[23] This interpretation fits well with the thought of the passage, since the terms used to evoke the punishment of Edom in verse 13 are borrowed from passages which express precisely the (unthinkable) overturning of the covenant, and associated benefits, with respect to Judah (*cf*. 7:34; 19:8; 22:5). It should be preferred to one which has no analogy elsewhere in the book, and which would be a curious mishandling of the passages in *Jeremiah* to which it evidently alludes (25:17ff., 29). Consequently, it is no basis for the view that the OAN enshrine a different understanding of Judah from that which otherwise prevails in the book.

We have now seen that the main arguments for regarding the OAN as inconsistent with important aspects of the theology of *Jeremiah* fall when due attention is paid to the wider structure of the book, and especially to the function in it of chapters 27 – 29. These observations are congruent with our general argument that the 'Book of Consolation' (the proper sequel of 27 – 29, as we have seen) stands at the heart of *Jeremiah*, and accounts for many of its features. It was that theology which rendered intelligible, for example, Jeremiah's promise of new, permanent institutions (33:14–26), even though such a promise stood in stark contrast with his earlier criticism of the cult (7:1–25).[24] In the same way, the 'Book of Consolation' provides the key to a proper

141

understanding of the OAN's function in the book. We are now in a position to elaborate this point by looking more closely at parts of the Babylonian oracles.

The Babylonian oracles

The delimitation of the component parts of the oracles is notoriously difficult, and has struck some commentators as having no system at all.[25] K. T. Aitken, however, has proposed that they are a 'well-ordered complex of structurally related elements', in six 'movements'.[26] While Aitken's analysis remains necessarily provisional, it is illuminating at important points. As a result of his enquiry, he claims that the structure of chapters 50 – 51 makes two main assertions, namely (i) that the situation of Judah will be radically changed (50:4–20; 51:34–44 – his movements A and E), and (ii) assurance to Judah that YHWH is indeed powerful to effect this change (50:33–46; 51:45–53 – movements C and F. B, 50:21–32, and D, 51:1–33, are subsidiary movements in his treatment, and in their different ways stand close to the themes of A to C as a whole). His movement A is interesting in particular for our purposes.

In Aitken's complex analysis, the statements (or 'ground-elements') of the various oracles are classified in three categories: *situation* (Babylon's past actions), *intervention* (YHWH's activity in changing the situation), and *outcome* (the new situation produced for Judah).[27] Aitken's treatment of 50:4–20 is especially illuminating. In that section, the ground-elements occur in a concentric pattern consisting of nine units. Thus, verses 4f. comprise the first unit (A), which corresponds to verses 19–20 (A'), not only in thought (*outcome* statements of restoration), but also in phraseology ('in those days and in that time', 4, 20). Similarly, verses 6–7 (B) correspond to verse 17 (B'), referring to Judah's *situation* (oppressed because of her sin), and also connected by similar phrasing ('my people have been lost sheep'/'Israel is a hunted sheep').[28]

Aitken has laid an important foundation for the interpretation of the passage in question with his understanding of the interplay of *situation* and *outcome* statements. More can be said, however, about the way in which the 'outcome', in this instance at least, is pictured. Our interest focuses on the elements A and A'. As *outcome* statements they throw the stress of the whole pericope on to Israel's restoration. (Christensen, incidentally, also remarked on the significance of 19f., as an evidence of the transformation of the OAN from war oracle to eschatological promise.)[29] The pairing of verses 4f. and 19f. invites a further observation, however. In verses 4f. the picture of restoration is conveyed through a repentant Israel. There are echoes, in a broad sense, of other passages where Israel is depicted as penitent, *viz.* 3:22b–24; 14:7–9. There are, furthermore, particular reminiscences of the 'Book of Consolation' (*e.g.* 'weeping', *cf.* 31:9, 15f.; 'they shall ask the way to Zion', *cf.* 30:17f.; 31:6, 12; 'everlasting covenant', *cf.* 33:14–26, itself an extrapolation of 31:31–34).[30] In other words, verses 4f. focus on that aspect of the 'Book of Consolation' which celebrates the penitent but joyful return of the exiles to their God and to Zion.

Verses 19f. also make connections with the 'Book of Consolation'. Most obviously, the idea of a pardoning which results in an absence of sin (20) echoes 31:34. Restoration to land is prominent here (19) as in the 'Book of Consolation', and indeed the emphasis on its richness and fertility is shared also (*cf.* 31:12–14). There are allusions to 'Ephraim' in both places (19, *cf.* 31:6, 18, 20). A hopeful 'remnant' idea is also held in common (20, *cf.* 31:7), two of the only three such occurrences in the book (*cf.* 23:3; other uses of the term 'remnant' either occur in threatening passages, or designate in a rather neutral way the community left in Palestine after the fall of Jerusalem, *e.g.* 6:9; 40:11).

More interesting than the affinities with the 'Book of Consolation' in themselves, however, is the dominant tone of the passage. It is set by the striking opening and closing statements of YHWH: 'I will restore . . .' and 'I will pardon . . .' The emphasis here, therefore, is in contrast with that in

143

verses 4f., and falls squarely on the activity of YHWH in the restoration of the people. The correspondence between verses 4f. and verses 19f., then, does not merely consist in their common drawing on the motifs of the 'Book of Consolation', but in its articulation of a central theological thought there, namely the relation between repentance and redemption in the future restoration. We saw, indeed, that one of the chief concerns of the 'Book of Consolation' was to address this theological topic, and found important formulations in regard to it in 31:31–34; 32:39f.[31] It seems that the Babylonian oracle in 50:4–20 has, in its own way, taken up this topic (as did, incidentally, chapters 37 – 44). Its method in doing so is particularly striking, for it appears to have leant especially on 31:7–20 for its ideas and phraseology, yet to have distributed them between its two framing passages (4f. and 19f.). (*Cf.* Aitken's idea, in pursuit of a different point, of a distribution of 'related thematic material' in his movements A and C of the oracles.)[32] Each also makes connections, directly or indirectly, with the central new covenant passage, 31:31–34. In this way, therefore, the oracle has built the theology of new covenant into its proclamation of a reversal in Israel's fortunes at the expense of its former oppressor. The passage in question is certainly the most striking example of this theologizing in the Babylon oracles. There is a further hint of a similar balancing of the two poles of the restoration theology of the 'Book of Consolation', however, in 51:36f., 45.

Promises of salvation to the nations

Having shown that the treatment of the great themes of OAN, namely the destinies of Judah/Israel and Babylon, is integrated into the broad sweep of chapters 25 – 51, with the 'Book of Consolation' at its theological hub, we can now consider that somewhat surprising feature of the OAN, the promises of salvation to certain of the nations, namely Egypt (46:26b), Moab (48:47), Ammon (49:6) and Elam (49:39).

These verses have often been suppressed by commentators as later additions to the prophecies, partly on the grounds that they do not all appear in LXX.[33] Holladay urges, additionally, that their universalism suggests 'a time well into the Persian period'.[34] And Rudolph attempts to show that the nations which receive these promises did later enjoy times of revival which explain these *post hoc* additions.[35]

There is, however, no compelling reason to deny these to the original OAN. The text-critical reason is not so strong as appears at first, because the phrase is present in LXX in the case of Elam (25:19 LXX). Furthermore, we have seen that there is no set pattern which we can expect OAN to take, and indeed that they can be used by prophets in surprising ways (as with Amos). Carroll, indeed, recognizes this point, allowing the promises of restoration to stand in the OAN as 'grace notes'.[36] We may add the observation that the idea of salvation for the nations is not absent from *Jeremiah*, having identified it as a minor theme in the theology of chapters 1 – 20 (see 3:17; 12:15f.; 16:19).[37]

The question remains, however, whether this theme in 46 – 49 is in conflict, as Carroll thinks, with what he sees as the nationalism of the Babylon oracles. It can be answered only in the context of the whole portrayal of Judah/Israel and the nations in *Jeremiah*, which, as we have seen, is characterized in its entirety by a great reversal. Do the promises to the nations fit within that scheme?

There is, in fact, a satisfying symmetry in the involvement of the nations with Judah in her redemption, following their involvement with her in her discomfiture at Babylon's hands. (46:28 may be seen as hyperbolic, and directed in any case effectively against Babylon.) This symmetry is enhanced by the use in the promise of restoration to Moab, Ammon and Elam (48:47; 49:6, 39) of the very phrase which was also used repeatedly of Judah and Israel in the 'Book of Consolation' (*viz. šaḇtî/'āšîḇ šᵉḇûṯ*; *cf.* 30:3 *etc.*, and above).[38] Furthermore, the logic of the proclamation first of judgment, then unexpectedly, of salvation, characterizes the promises to Israel/Judah in the 'Book of Consolation' at, for example,

30:12–17; 32:26–41. The pointed exclusion of Babylon from the hope extended here to certain of the nations also helps to create a reversal from the situation found in chapters 27 – 29, in which Babylon alone was triumphant. (The denial of hope to other nations in 46 – 49 is not so easily explained. The 'hope' editing has evidently not been systematic, of course, as the divergences between MT and LXX show.)

The observations just made presuppose a thought-out relationship among the various parts of 25 – 51, for which we have been arguing. Our remarks so far on this structure may now be taken further, partly in response to Carroll's observation, correct in itself, of parallels between *Jeremiah* 30f. and 50f. In noticing these, however, he went on to claim that 'the differences between the cycles are more significant than the shared motif of restoration', on the grounds that the former laid no stress on the defeat of Israel's enemies.[39] Though having affinities, therefore, the two blocks of material were independent traditions. When we consider the two sections as parts of a broader developing picture in the book the matter stands differently. The relevant material forms a concentric pattern:

A Chapter 25 — Babylon as scourge of the nations; Judah punished by Babylon's depredation, and seventy-year exile; other nations also punished by same hand; the punishment of Babylon (25:12, a minor theme here).

B Chapters 27 – 29 — The motif of Judah's bearing the punishment in common with other nations is continued; Jeremiah is transformed into a salvation-prophet, by means of the idea of a seventy-year exile.

C Chapters 30 – 33 — Salvation for Judah/Israel is proclaimed.

B' Chapters Jeremiah as salvation-prophet for Israel and
46 – 49 Judah; other nations involved in the salvation-
prophecy, by means of the motif of their
restored fortunes (adapted from C).

A' Chapters The salvation of Judah and Israel is con-
50 – 51 tinued, and the punishment of Babylon is now
taken up as a major theme.

This concentric pattern, which of course organizes the
material in question from only one point of view, risks over-
simplifying even in respect of our immediate point. (For
example, certain motifs are carried over from A to B and
from B' to A', as the table above shows.) Nevertheless, it
reveals certain important correspondences. The relationship
between ABB'A' shows that the problem of Judah/Israel,
Babylon and the nations has received careful treatment on
the broad plan of the book. So too has the idea of Jeremiah
as a salvation-prophet. The 'Book of Consolation' (C in our
pattern) is the important catalyst in the theological discourse
which handles all these matters. The transformation of Jeremiah and the changes in the fates of Judah/Israel, of the
nations and of Babylon are all intelligible in terms of
YHWH's new covenant with his people.

The pattern also shows why it is mistaken to worry about
whether the similarities between the OAN and chapters 30f.
are more or less significant than the differences. Chapters
30f. do not handle the nations theme in themselves, because
that is not their function in this discourse. They are nevertheless the fulcrum in a complex theological whole, which
embraces the question of the nations.

Conclusions

Our treatment of the OAN serves to show that, here as on
other occasions, interpretations which claim to have seen
disharmonious diversity between parts of the book of

Jeremiah have understood it, wrongly I believe, to consist of independent parts which themselves are static in their theology and in their portraits of the prophet. On the contrary, the book, as we have been trying to unfold its developing logic, has given us a number of clues to its own view that nothing here is static. Nor should we expect this in prophetic books. The perspective on *Jeremiah* which we have been advocating in relation to the OAN may be reinforced by the fact that a multi-faceted view of the conqueror-nation is not without precedent in a prophetic book. In Isaiah, Assyria is seen first as scourge of Israel, then as rebel against YHWH, in respect of its military campaigns against the people (Is. 10:5–19). That passage may, indeed, be seen as a theologizing of just the kind of reversal we find in relation to Babylon in *Jeremiah*. *Jeremiah* therefore is not only individual in its use of the OAN form, but also, in this respect, firmly within the prophetic tradition.

The specific results of our investigation of the OAN are that the relationship between chapters 27 – 29 and 50 – 51 depends very largely upon the reversal which is pictured, rather thoroughly, between the two sections. That reversal embraces the destinies of Judah/Israel, Babylon and the nations. The transformation in the role of the prophet, which is achieved in chapters 27 – 29, is instrumental in realizing the reversal, and the position of the 'Book of Consolation' between the two 'Babylonian' sections also plays a crucial part. It follows, incidentally, that the interpretation offered here, by which the OAN, including the Babylonian oracles, are integrated fully into the thought of the book, works best when the MT order is followed, rather than the LXX order, *i.e.* when the OAN occupy a final and climactic place in the book.[40]

CHAPTER EIGHT

Jeremiah the prophet

Since the introduction to our study we have suspended the question whether or how far the book of *Jeremiah* may be attributable to the prophet Jeremiah. This was because of the method of approaching the subject. At that early stage of the book, we noticed, in a preliminary way, certain affinities among Deuteronomy, Hosea and *Jeremiah*, and an important difference between these on the one hand and DtH on the other. We then approached the question of the relationship between *Jeremiah* and the Deuteronomistic corpus by means of a study of the book as a whole. This, I think, has both resolved some of the inner tensions which have been felt to prove the disparate authorship of the book, and has shown the difficulty of regarding it as a Deuteronomistic product. The tendency of our study to this point, furthermore, has supported our contention that the book is substantially the product of one mind. We are now in a position to take further our early observation that *Jeremiah* resembled Hosea in certain respects, by asking whether the lines of thought we have now seen in *Jeremiah* may be considered to fall within the parameters of the Israelite prophetic tradition. If so, it will be the more plausible to maintain that the mind behind the book is indeed that of Jeremiah. Our investigation will focus in due course once again on Hosea, but will also cast its net somewhat wider.

Jeremiah and the prophetic tradition

To question the authenticity of Jeremiah's words is partly to ask whether they stand plausibly within a tradition of prophetic thought. One must say 'partly' by way of a caveat, for it would be wrong to preclude the possibility of novelty and individuality in Jeremiah. If, however, the belief that *Jeremiah* is Deuteronomistic has over-emphasized *Jeremiah*'s affinities with DtH, it has correspondingly underplayed its affinities with classical prophecy. This has happened, not because the prophets have not been studied carefully enough, but because the debate about *Jeremiah* and the Deuteronomist has involved a certain estimate of what constituted their message. To place Jeremiah in relation to the prophetic tradition, therefore, requires us first to ask what the prophetic tradition was.

Recent discussion of the prophetic movement has laid some stress on what is called the 'Ephraimite' tradition. This consists of the theological stream that is thought to have been nurtured in northern Israel, and deposited chiefly in the putative E document, the traditions surrounding Samuel and Elijah, and the northern prophets, especially Hosea, and in Deuteronomy.[1] The affinities between Hosea and Deuteronomy are well documented.[2] So too are the similarities between these and *Jeremiah*. Unexpectedly, perhaps, Judean *Jeremiah* belongs to the 'Ephraimite' tradition, for reasons to which we shall return.

The affinities between these literary deposits is not a new discovery. Von Rad's studies in Deuteronomy led him to think of it as a revival, within cultic circles, of amphictyonic traditions, though he was reluctant to characterize the proclamation nurtured by these circles as prophetic.[3] This perspective was modified by Muilenburg and Kraus, who took a more positive view of the role of cultic prophets in perpetrating the preaching of Deuteronomy, and saw them, indeed, as fulfilling a function analogous to that of Moses *vis-à-vis* the covenant.[4] In this way the essence of the northern tradition, with its affinities between Deuteronomy and the prophets, is seen in terms of its debt to the Mosaic covenant, deriving from pre-monarchical Israel.[5]

The similarities which these literary deposits bear to each other are by no means illusory. To notice them, however, is only the beginnings of tormenting questions. Is the relationship between Deuteronomy and the prophets one of simple continuity? Are there not, rather, important differences between the prophets and Deuteronomy? And if so, how does one disentangle the separate influences of Deuteronomy and prophecy on the form of the prophetic books as we now have them? In addition we may ask whether the theological stream in question is truly 'Ephraimite', or whether the Old Testament prophets of north and south were not more similar than they were different, because of important shared elements in their heritage.

Prophecy in the older traditions (E)

By the 'older traditions' is meant the literature which is admitted to pre-date Deuteronomy. The first problem with treating them is to determine their limits. For example, there has been some tendency to deny the existence of the E document as a separate source,[6] partly as a result of a tendency to treat more and more of the Old Testament literature as Deuteronomistic. If, however, the Pentateuchal literature which has traditionally been ascribed to E (and often still is[7]) is allowed some antiquity, there is evidence of considerable interest in prophecy in it (*e.g.* Nu. 11:25ff.; 12). It will be of greater interest for us if those traditions reveal some of the features that we see in Jeremiah's work. They do indeed promote the view that the prophet is intercessor (Ex. 32; Nu. 21:4ff.). And if the decalogue, together with the Book of the Covenant, and Joshua 24, be reckoned to E,[8] then that document's interest in prophecy stands in a broad context of covenantal theology. Furthermore, Deuteronomy 32, also sometimes assigned to E,[9] has a view of Israel's moral incapacity that has many affinities with the preaching of

151

Jeremiah, and sees not only judgment on the chosen nation for her sin, but also beyond judgment to a salvation (36) which vindicates her, while bringing wrath on her (and YHWH's) enemies.

The value of a discussion of E in itself, however, is necessarily qualified by the need to discuss in the same connection the relation of E to Deuteronomy and the Deuteronomist. The date of individual passages can hardly be decided apart from the general view which is taken of that relationship. Where the Deuteronomist increases, E must decrease – and with it the argument for the existence of an ethical religion, based on the dual possibilities enshrined in covenantal theology, before the classical prophets. One clear result, however, of modern thinking on Israel's religion in the period of the monarchy is the extreme difficulty of distinguishing successfully between the relative deposits of E and the Deuteronomist. The problem was felt by Clements in his authoritative survey of Pentateuchal problems.[10] And it arises persistently in R. R. Wilson's attempt to recover the life-settings and actual speech of the prophets, where Wilson, all the time admitting the methodological difficulty, tends to allow the maximum to the 'Ephraimite prophets' wherever he can.[11]

Hosea

Surer footholds, nevertheless, may be found in the relationship between *Jeremiah* and Hosea. Affinities between the two prophecies have long been noted, and are important for our study because Hosea represents a clearly earlier stage in the prophetic tradition than *Jeremiah* and because much recent study of the book allows a high degree of correspondence between its contents and the theology of the prophet himself. Just as, in our introduction, we considered the relationship between *Jeremiah* and DtH under the heads of 'style' and 'theology', we shall also address the relationship between *Jeremiah* and Hosea in the same way.

a. Style

We have already shown that the prose of *Jeremiah* was no longer a safe index of the extent of Deuteronomistic influence upon it. The converse can now be argued, namely that Jeremiah could have inherited a tradition of prophetic discourse which embraced both prose and poetry, and which indeed was of such a character as to question the clean antithesis between those two modes of discourse which used to be taken for granted. The argument in principle was made with great dexterity in the important work of J. L. Kugel. Kugel finds such scholarly recourses as 'rhythmical prose', 'unmetrical poetry' and 'parallelistic prose', used of certain kinds of Old Testament discourse, to be symptomatic of a failure to read that discourse according to its true character. Rather than seeing prose and poetry as two distinct phenomena, he argues for a continuum in Hebrew discourse, within which some parts are more, and some less, highly organized, according to the extent to which they exhibit features which mark them out as 'special'. Such features include those which have traditionally marked out poetry, namely parallelism (though he prefers to call it 'seconding') and terseness. Furthermore, greater and lesser degrees of organization, he believes, can appear within the same text. This he regards as a better explanation of the irregularities of texts which, according to the traditional ways of representing them in both English and Hebrew Bibles, can look ragged. The ragged look is a product of wrongly imported categories, and leads in turn to an impression, before critical reading has begun, of inherent disunity.[12]

Closer to our immediate concerns is the commentary of F. I. Andersen and D. N. Freedman (A-F) on Hosea (which appeared a year earlier than Kugel's book). While there are important theoretical differences between the two works, A-F make many similar observations to those of Kugel. They do not resort to extensive emendation of the text of Hosea in the cause of reconstructing an original text according to criteria of strict poetic style. Rather, they conclude, not for

Hosea alone but of a 'prophetic literary pattern, characteristic at least of the eighth-century prophets':

> This style or quality of literature does not fall obviously into either of the classical categories of prose or poetry, but seems to be a mixture, in which the parts are blended rather than being separated either by form or content.[13]

A-F's investigation shows that there is a variation within Hosea in the extent to which prose markers appear. Their greater frequency in chapters 1 – 3 than in 4 – 14 leads them to think that, while 4 – 14 stem directly from the prophet, 1 – 3, though deriving from his teaching, have been put together by someone else.[14] Nevertheless, their assessment of the authenticity of the prophecy as a whole is high.

Before leaving the matter of Hosea's style, a word is in place about the narratives of chapters 1 and 3. These passages fall clearly towards the 'ordinary', rather than the 'elevated', end of the scale of Hebrew discourse. Critical discussion of these passages, however, has centred not on their style, but on their relation to each other. Is the woman of chapter 3 the Gomer of chapter 1? What is the sequence of the two reported events in the prophet's life? That the accounts relate to Hosea's own experiences, and that chapter 3 at least derives directly from him, is scarcely doubted (even if some have sought ways of understanding the experience in ways other than the literal). The 'prosaic' character of the discourse has, in this case, not entered the discussion. Rather, chapter 3 is viewed by Wolff, Mays, A-F and others as a prophetic symbolic action. Westerman too classes it with other prophetic narratives which he sees as reporting parabolic actions, a phenomenon from 'the early days of prophecy'.[15]

The arguments about Hosea which we have thus aired can be said to belong to a general tendency in modern discussion to estimate highly the authenticity of most of the book. The relevance to our study of *Jeremiah* is that it establishes broad stylistic parameters within the prophetic tradition. These parameters relate both to the kind of speech available to a prophet to use, and to the possibility of a rather 'ordinary' kind of discourse (typical in fact of narrative) in connection with the account of events in the prophet's life. Naturally, observations of this sort do not force the conclusion that all parts of *Jeremiah* are authentic without more ado. The study of the characteristics of a tradition does not preclude a prophet's individuality; nor could conformity to a tradition prove authenticity. The considerations we have just brought to bear, however, form a further part of the general case for locating much or most of the discourse of *Jeremiah* in the life and times of Jeremiah.

b. Theology

In our examination of the theology of *Jeremiah* we showed the coherence of what appeared to be competing theological positions in the unfolding dynamic of the book. It could thus be maintained that a call to repentance as well as promise of a wholly new future, dependent on YHWH's initiative in creating his people's capacity to obey him, had a place in the book alongside the threats of judgment. The coherence was established by a prophetic logic which first uncovered the people's inability to respond, then met that inability with a new understanding of the relationship between human response and the divine initiative (elaborated in the 'Book of Consolation'). Our question now is whether the various parts of the message of *Jeremiah* can be found also in the ministry of Hosea. In this way we shall answer the question, not only whether the book of *Jeremiah* has coherence, but whether its message as a whole may have emanated from the experience of the prophet.

An essential topic in the pursuit of the comparison is that of repentance. We have discussed above the question whether Jeremiah actually preached a message of repentance, and found that he almost certainly did so, even though the book as it stands constitutes a reflection back upon that preaching in the knowledge that the change of heart did not in fact come about. It is time now to broaden the question, and ask whether, in preaching repentance, Jeremiah stood within the prophetic tradition.

The question whether repentance belongs at all in the earliest stages of prophecy merits discussion in itself. Westermann saw the judgment oracle against the individual as primary in the development of prophecy. The form was patient of expansions and variations, but had no place for hope. The call to repentance, with its suggestion that doom might after all be avoided, arose only in what Westermann calls the 'Dissolution of the Form'. He observes this occurring in Haggai and Zechariah (*e.g.* Zc. 1:3). Their adoption of this new thing in prophecy is a result of the exile, which carried in its train a reinterpretation of pre-exilic prophecy. The main examples of this reinterpretation are found in *Jeremiah* and Ezekiel. This transformation of what he thinks of as the properly prophetic form he characterizes as Deuteronomistic. Its particular effect is that 'the prophetic proclamation is no longer formed as a concrete accusation, but rather as a call to repentance, and in fact (5) a call to repentance that is based on a conditional announcement of salvation'.[16] The influence of Westermann has been far-reaching, and traces of it can be found, for example, in Thiel's denial of *Jeremiah* 7:3 to the prophet.[17]

Westermann has not gone unchallenged, however. H. Weippert has brought further light to bear upon the subject from extra-biblical sources. She takes issue directly with Thiel for a too rigid distinction between the theology of the Deuteronomist and that of the prophets. In particular she argues against his view that 'alternatives' characterize the former to the exclusion of the latter, *i.e.* the kind of preaching which holds out different possibilities depending on response. She adduces in favour of her view texts from Deir 'Alla in which she finds that the common topos of curse and blessing in ANE treaties is also present within a prophetic framework. This is highly significant for the understanding of biblical prophecy in general, because the analogy suggests (though it alone can hardly prove it) that biblical prophecy is precisely a preaching of the blessing and curse already known from biblical covenant arrangements, a position which is widely challenged today.[18]

To come to the biblical corpus itself, the evidence from Hosea is of the first importance, for his message of judgment also knows of the possibility of repentance. Straight calls to repent in Hosea come at 12:7(6) and 14:2f. (1f.). 6:1 can also be regarded as such a call because when taken together with 5:15 it amounts to the same thing. These occurrences of the idea are in addition to those where it is said, for example, that 'Israel *shall* [my italics] return . . .' (3:5, *cf.* 14:7). Indeed, there is further evidence that repentance is an issue for Hosea, albeit indirectly, in passages such as 6:11b; 7:10, 16. Failures of the sort recorded here are not Hosea's final word, however. The climax of the theme comes in chapter 14 with its two-fold exhortation to 'return', and the assurances that YHWH will 'heal their faithlessness' (5[4]: the expression used, *'erpā' meš̌ûḇāṭām*, is related to the verb *š̌ûḇ*, 'return' or 'repent') and that his anger will 'turn' from them.

There can be little doubt that the repentance theme is embedded deep in the record of the ministry of Hosea. Most modern commentators find no strong objections to the authenticity of the passages in question. Even where 6:1–3 is regarded as a priestly liturgy, it is found to fit well into the prophecy, and to cohere with Hosea's basic message.[19] It could equally, however, be free composition by the prophet. Wolff has also defended 12:7(6) against the suggestion (of Westermann's) that it represents later parenetic elaboration of the prophet's message, on the grounds of its similarity to Hosea's diction elsewhere.[20] It seems therefore that the theology of repentance can only be denied to Hosea by doing some violence to the text.

What is even more significant about the repentance idea in Hosea than its mere presence is the fact that, in its range and flexibility, it anticipates *Jeremiah* closely. As in *Jeremiah*, it is used rhetorically to produce certain contrasts. Thus, the 'returning' of the people in 6:1 balances that of YHWH in 5:15: he will return to his place, until they return to him.

Then in chapter 14, the appeal to the people to 'return' (2–4 [1–3]) is matched once again by a turning of YHWH, this time from his anger (5[4]). We may compare the similar usage of the verb *šûḇ* in *Jeremiah* (4:1, 8).

The similarity with *Jeremiah* goes further, however, for verses 2–4 (1–3) are followed by a quite different kind of statement in 5–9 (4–8). Here YHWH, not content apparently, to wait for the repentance asked for, takes matters upon himself, and says: '*I* [my italics] will heal their faithlessness (*mᵉšûḇāṭām*) . . .' (The phrase is identical with that in *Jeremiah* 3:22.) The juxtaposition of these two sections has been variously understood. Some have thought that YHWH's declaration in 5–9 (4–8) was a response to that of penitent Israel in 2–4 (1–3). In contrast, G. I. Emmerson considers the two passages to be unintegrated, the context of the salvation oracle being no guide to the theology of Hosea himself.[21]

In fact, however, the tension which we may admit to exist in the juxtaposition of 14:2–4 (1–3) and 5–9 (4–8) is better regarded as belonging in a fundamental way to the message of Hosea. The question is whether a call to repent is compatible with the declaration that it is YHWH in the end who must effect the desired change of heart in Israel. The book of Hosea shows, I believe, that there is a theological compatibility here, even if not a strictly logical one. This is because, together with the appeal to repent in Hosea, there are statements which imply that Israel will not do so. 7:10, 16 are examples. This fact produces a conflict. YHWH would save Israel; repentance is a precondition of salvation, but the condition is not fulfilled. Must the axe fall therefore? The answer comes in the famous 11:8ff. YHWH cannot cast 'Ephraim' off, because of his own nature. (Notice how the motif of 'returning', used with an ironic twist, 5, 7, belongs to the logic that leads up to the climax in 8ff.) How then shall the conflict be resolved, if not in the obvious way, namely by YHWH's withholding of the desired salvation? Hosea's answer is that which we have observed in chapter 14, namely that YHWH himself will effect the requisite change of heart in Israel. If that is a conundrum it is nevertheless the final word of the book of Hosea on the matter.

Hosea 14:2–9 (1–8), in fact, neatly focuses Hosea's understanding of Israel's future with YHWH. The call to repent in the earlier verses, far from being an attempt to superimpose a theology of repentance on that of YHWH's initiative, is rather a summation of that which has led to the declaration of YHWH in 5 (4). The effect, in the context of the whole book of Hosea, is precisely to affirm the need for that initiative in the light of Israel's chronic failure to repent. Paradoxically, of course, the call to repent also continues to function precisely as such. The divine initiative will not extinguish the appeal.

One further aspect of the theology of 'return' in Hosea remains to be considered. We have established that the salvation of Israel, in Hosea, requires an initiative of YHWH because of the incapacity of the people to repent. The question remains, however, how the prophet thinks that salvation will come about, and indeed whether he takes it to lie beyond a judgment and exile.

There are a number of indications that this is indeed his view. The section 5:15 – 6:3 pictures a 'binding up' that follows a 'wounding', and this sequence of ideas may thus be said to belong to the world of Hosea's thought. For more explicit intimations of exile and restoration, however, appeal can be made to other passages. First, the idea of a movement through judgment to salvation underlies Hosea 1 and 2. The repudiations of Israel in 1:6–7 are turned around in 2:1–3 (1:10 – 2:1). The language of 'gathering' (2:1) suggests a returning to the land after dissipation among the nations. The use of the verb elsewhere in Hosea (8:10; 9:6) suggests exile. The return from exile announced here, therefore, relates to the theology of anticipated judgment by exile elsewhere in the book, as well as at 1:6–7. Affinities between 2:1–3 and Ezekiel 37:15–22 have been taken as evidence of an exilic origin of the former.[22] Wolff, however, balances the point by observing affinities with Hosea's own thought and use of language, and considers it at least uncertain how far the verses may come from Hosea himself.[23]

The situation is more straightforward with 2:25 (23), which belongs in a unified group of sayings in 2:18–25. (The formal unity consists in the sayings' character as divine speeches characterizing 'that day'.)[24] Here, the threat of 1:6–7 is once again reversed, now by means of a 'sowing' in the land. The picture of judgment and salvation again implies exile and restoration, in a passage which is widely attributed to Hosea.

Hosea 3 forms a natural sequel to 2. Wolff considers it older than chapter 1, which it did not originally presuppose, and closely connected in terms of transmission, as well as theme, with chapter 2.[25] It is, however, a composition of Hosea. The chapter announces a period when Israel will be deprived of her institutions, followed by one in which, by her repentance, these are restored.

Further evidence comes from Hosea 11. We have already had cause to refer to this chapter because of its middle section (8–9), where YHWH recoils from acting in judgment on his people. A reading of the whole chapter shows, however, that this is not to be understood to mean that no punishment will fall at all. Rather, the passage is sandwiched between an affirmation that

> They shall return to the land of Egypt,
>   and Assyria shall be their king, (11:5, *cf.* 8:13)

and

> . . . his sons shall come trembling from the west;
>   they shall come trembling like birds from Egypt,
>   and like doves from the land of Assyria;
>   and I will return them to their homes, says the LORD.
>   (11:10c–11)

It follows from the construction of the chapter, therefore, that 8–9 should not be taken to mean that YHWH will not punish at all, but rather that his purposes are not ultimately the destruction of his people. His disposition to save, rather, will be manifested in a redemption from the judgment of exile. Chapter 11 therefore has affinities with Hosea 2 (with which it also shares the formal feature *n^e'um Yahweh*, oracle of the LORD – though Wolff insists that the two passages show differences in their history of transmission).[26] It is closest to 2:1–3, 18–25, because the decision of YHWH's to save is not motivated by repentance on Israel's part. In this it also stands close to 14:5, with which it therefore brings the theme of return to the land into proximity.

The parallels with *Jeremiah* are thus quite extensive, suggesting indeed, that both books are the reflective, digested accounts of the respective prophets' ministries. The plays on the root *šûḇ* are similar to those which we observed above (chapter 1) in our treatment of the repentance theme in *Jeremiah* 3. So too is the relationship between the usages. Where YHWH says 'I will heal their faithlessness' in *Jeremiah* 3:22, it immediately follows an appeal to repent (same verse). The logic is therefore exactly analogous to that which we have just observed in Hosea 14. Indeed the whole logic which undergirds *Jeremiah* is also found here. The story of *Jeremiah*, as we saw, was a story of Judah's moral incapacity laid bare. There was, consequently, an inevitable conflict between YHWH's need to judge the sin of his people and his desire to save them. His agonized dilemma was depicted in *Jeremiah* at 31:20, which finds its counterpart in Hosea at 11:8ff. (The echoes of Hosea in *Jeremiah* 31:20 are in fact quite extensive. The chosen nation is referred to as both Ephraim and YHWH's son: *cf.* Hosea 11:1, 9.) The passion of emotional involvement is common to both. The expression 'yearns for' is strongly anthropomorphic (or better, anthropopathic), based on a word (*mē'ay*), meaning 'bowels', and designating the seat of the deepest human emotions. This too stands close to the human-like agony of Hosea 11:8ff. The terms of the final declaration of the verse, finally, with its double use of the verb *rḥm* (also based on human organs and similarly related to emotions) are strongly reminiscent of the language of Hosea 1:6–8; 2:25. The outcome of the story in *Jeremiah* was

YHWH's declared intent to take a new initiative in the relationship between himself and the people. So it is also in Hosea. Here as there, failure issues in a new hope newly based. Hosea knows the new covenant in all but name.

A further implication of the close theological affinities between the two prophetic works is that the relationship between them is more intimate than that which exists between either of them and DtH. We noticed above (introduction) how close *Jeremiah* stands to Deuteronomy 30:1–10, because of the theology according to which YHWH would do a new work in the hearts of his people, and they would be able to return in penitent faith to their land. By the same token, both *Jeremiah* and Deuteronomy 30:1–10 were distinct from the theology in Kings. This emerges most forcefully from a comparison of Deuteronomy 30:1–10 with 1 Kings 8:46–53, where the prayer of Solomon seems to typify the hope of DtH for Israel beyond the exile, and in which there is no mention of a return to the land.

It is clear, therefore, that both *Jeremiah* and Hosea stand close to Deuteronomy 30:1–10, but differ from DtH. *Jeremiah*, furthermore, stands firmly in a tradition which goes back to Hosea, and is therefore properly prophetic. That prophetic tradition, however, is in line with theologizing which we have found within the book of Deuteronomy. These observations, therefore, support the view that the prophetic movement had important affinities with Deuteronomy. Deuteronomy, furthermore, is in some respects at least, closer to the prophets than to DtH.

All this is true, of course, only if Deuteronomy 30:1–10 can be regarded as properly part of Deuteronomy. In most critical discussion, however, it is thought to have other roots. Yet it has not been easy for scholars to find a suitable place for it within any of the standard categories with which they try to explain the literature that bears the marks of Deuteronomy. Rather, it is often placed in a category of its own, as a piece which simply reflects the hopes of certain people in the exilic period. Yet, because of the passage's closeness in thought to Hosea, it would seem that to assign it to a class of its own is to multiply entities unnecessarily. Deuteronomy 30:1–10 may, in fact, be regarded as one of those parts of Deuteronomy which resembles aspects of the theology of Hosea and *Jeremiah*. One consequence of this is that approaches to *Jeremiah* which attempt to minimize the relationship between *Jeremiah* and Deuteronomy in the interests of showing the authenticity of the *Jeremiah* prose underestimate the closeness of *Jeremiah* to Deuteronomy, and fail to distinguish adequately between the theology and interests of Deuteronomy and DtH.[27]

In conclusion it can be said that *Jeremiah*, seen as a whole, can be plausibly placed within a genuinely prophetic tradition, which also has links with Deuteronomy. Our study of Hosea played an important part in leading to this conclusion. It is one of the more curious characteristics of the whole area of study before us that scholars are prepared to allow a great deal to Hosea in terms of a theology of repentance and of a return to the land beyond an exile, based on a new action of YHWH's. Yet there is a tremendous reluctance to extend these very things to the later prophet Jeremiah. This is a tension residing within current critical orthodoxy, maintained, I think, because of the resilience of certain favourite tenets of *Jeremiah* criticism. The tension will almost certainly be resolved one way or the other. R. P. Carroll, who is well aware of it, would clearly like to see it resolved by a more sceptical approach to Hosea.[28] The present argument has tended to the other alternative, a return to a more positive assessment of Jeremiah's role in the book that bears his name.

Prophetic tradition : north and south

To argue, as we have done, that *Jeremiah* can reasonably be located within a prophetic tradition, raises a number of further questions. If *Jeremiah* stands in a tradition that is best exemplified by the northern prophet Hosea, does it follow that his roots are specifically northern, in distinction from

163

prophecy as it was known in the south? Muilenburg, in putting his case for a distinctive northern prophetic tradition, held that those prophets (like Micaiah or Isaiah) whose messages originated in visions of a 'Divine Council' stood in a different tradition.[29] R. R. Wilson accepts the basic difference, and attaches some importance to the terms typically used for northern and southern prophets, *viz. nābî'* and *hōzeh* respectively.[30] The term *hozeh*, he argues, itself suggests that the southern prophet was characterized by receiving his messages in some kind of vision form.[31] Petersen is rightly more cautious about building a theory of the actual meaning of words on an etymological basis,[32] and criticizes studies which attempt to do so, on the grounds that they are both wrongly based and inconclusive.[33] Valid distinctions, he believes, can be made only by means of the role-theory which he himself tries to apply. The result of his own investigation, however, is that there is indeed a significant difference between the use of the terms *nābî'* and *hōzeh*, the former representing usage in the north, the latter in the south.[34]

Petersen's role-theory argument depends on observations about the occurrences and meaning of the terms in question in the prophetic books. He examines a number of key passages, and concludes that the two terms were believed, by those who used them, to mean different things. (Certain passages in which the two are almost certainly synonymous, or in which *nābî'* is used of southern prophets, *e.g.* Is. 29:10; Am. 2:11f.; 3:7f., are ruled out of the enquiry because they are regarded as secondary.) Those passages bear examination.

The first is Micah 3:5–8. This passage is of interest because it is critical of *n^ebî'îm*, *hōzîm* and indeed *qōs^emîm* (diviners) also. Petersen's conclusion about the passage is that, because it is an attack upon improper manipulation of YHWH's word and vision, it 'affords us little leverage on the distinction between the various prophetic titles'.[35] The reason for this, however, may equally be that Micah is not thinking of clearly distinguishable groups at all. It is true that the oracle not only uses three terms for those who make known the mind of

YHWH but also the abstract nouns ḥāzôn (vision) and qᵉsôm (divination). There is no suggestion, however, that the activities indicated by the abstract nouns are associated directly with separate groups identified by the corresponding names. Indeed the terms ḥāzôn and qᵉsôm occur within a part of the passage in which only the nᵉbî'îm are so far in view (5–6). The evidence of Micah 3:5–8 suggests, if anything, that the names for prophetic figures do not indicate consciously different usages of the terms.

More significant for Petersen is Amos 7:12–15. Here, King Amaziah says to the unwelcome southerner:

'O seer (ḥōzeh), go, flee away to the land of Judah, and eat bread there, and prophesy (tinnābē') there' (12)

to which Amos retorts:

'I am no prophet (nābî'), nor a prophet's son . . .' (14)

Petersen deduces from this exchange that both Amaziah and Amos regard the term ḥōzeh as appropriate for Amos, and that they further agree that the term nābî' is inappropriate.[36] The interpretation fits neatly with the theory, espoused by Petersen, that the different terms were current in the south and north respectively. The meaning can then be taken to be as follows: Amaziah uses the term ḥōzeh advisedly, because it marks Amos out as one who may have a legitimate role in the south, but certainly none here in the north, where prophets are nᵉbî'îm. Amos then agrees that he is not, or was not, a nābî', but counters Amaziah by appealing to a call of YHWH that he should 'prophesy (tinnābē') to my people Israel' (15).

This interpretation, however, is cogent only if the more general theory is first accepted. In fact, Amos could be repudiating Amaziah's description of him as a ḥōzeh, by denying that he is a nābî'. In this case, as with the Micah passage, there is no significant difference between the terms. Rather the reverse; they are regarded as synonyms.

With the verb *nb'*, Petersen's case runs into some difficulty. His argument appears to depend on the assumption that Amos claims a newly established right to act as *nābî'* on the grounds that YHWH has commissioned him to prophesy (*tinnābē'*). Yet his whole attempt to force a difference between *nābî* and *ḥōzeh* depends on the view that the verb *nb'* does not correspond exclusively to the noun *nābî'*, but is used appropriately of the activities of both *nābî'* and *ḥōzeh*.[37] In this passage then, crucial for Petersen's theory, there is simply not enough evidence for it.

Petersen's argument against equating *nābî* and *ḥōzeh* proceeds otherwise largely by regarding certain passages as secondary (*e.g.* Am. 2:10–13; 3:7).[38] Our purpose would not be greatly enhanced by arguing over these. One further contention of his may be questioned, however, namely his explanation of the occurrence of *nābî* in some of the southern prophets. In this connection he points out that allusions to the *nābî* in the southern prophets are always pejorative, *e.g.* Isaiah 3:2; 28:7 (these in addition to Micah 3:5–8),[39] while in Hosea he is always *persona grata* (4:5 being secondary).[40] Once again the argument fails to convince, however. The fact that the *nᵉbî'îm* are spoken of coolly by the southern prophets does not imply that *nᵉbî'îm*, in contrast to the *ḥōzîm*, do not belong in the south. In fact, in Isaiah 3:2 the strong implication is that the *nābî'* is one who has been, and might be expected to be, a pillar of society. This is the force of the oracle in question, rather than that any of the terms used should be judged negatively in and of themselves.[41] The same is true in 28:7. Furthermore, as we have seen, the *ḥōzeh* can come in for criticism from a southern prophet too (Micah 3:7). And even if Hosea is largely positive in his allusions to the *nᵉbî'îm*, Jeremiah, for all the allegedly northern influence upon him, is not (2:26; 6:13).

In sum, the facts do not support the contention of both Wilson and Petersen that the *nābî'* is a typically northern phenomenon, while the *ḥōzeh* is typically southern. For perspective, however, it must be added that both Petersen and Wilson have some understanding of continuity between north and south as regards prophecy. Wilson generally polarizes much less than Petersen, even though he broadly accepts Muilenburg's schema.[42] Petersen himself regards both *nābî'* and *ḥōzeh* as 'central morality prophets', functioning in ways that are similar, but merely using different symbol systems.[43] His contribution to the debate is considerable, especially because of his warnings about misplaced reliance on etymology in attempting to distinguish between roles,[44] and his related perception that the role labels *nābî'* and *ḥōzeh* 'do not refer essentially to distinctive modes of revelation'.[45]

Southern influences on *Jeremiah*

The discussion about the affinities of *Jeremiah* goes wider than a consideration of the prophetic names, however, and indeed, than *Jeremiah*'s similarities with Hosea. In fact, the tendency to associate *Jeremiah* with the northern prophets has obscured the points which the book has in common with southern prophetic books. Of course, the question is complicated by the supposition that prophetic books in general have been subjected to later revision by Judahite groups. This renders problematical the attempt to uncover traits that were actually present in southern pre-exilic prophecy, rather than simply having been superimposed on it from an actual source in the northern-Deuteronomic nexus. Nevertheless, certain observations about the possible continuity between southern prophecy and *Jeremiah* are in place.

A first rather general comparison concerns the oracles against the nations (chapters 46 – 51 MT) in which *Jeremiah* possesses what appears to be a characteristic typical of southern prophecy, appearing also in Isaiah, Amos, Ezekiel and Zephaniah, but not in Hosea.

More particularly, the book of Amos shares a number of features with *Jeremiah*. First, Amos has four visions (7:1 – 8:3), all introduced by the same phrase ('Thus the LORD God showed me'), and belonging within a certain line of thought.

We notice first a formal similarity between the fourth vision in particular and one which Jeremiah received. The vision is of a basket of summer fruit (*qayiṣ*), which prompts an oracle about the end (*qēṣ*) that has come upon Israel (8:2). This is reminiscent of Jeremiah's rod of almond (1:11–12), both because of the form of the exchange between YHWH and the prophet, and because of the use of the play on words (*šāqēd*/*šōqēd*).

Second, the line of thought within which the visions appear is relevant. The section 7:1 – 8:3 concerns the silencing of prophecy in Israel, and the judgment which follows in its train. Amos is portrayed in the first two visions as the intercessor (2–3, 5–6). Thus far, indeed, his intercession is effective. In the third and fourth visions there is no such answered prayer; the judgment on Judah appears the more inevitable, and the oracle following the vision of the basket of fruit has an air of finality about it. Furthermore, Amos is prohibited by King Amaziah from prophesying (12–13), and this rejection of the word of YHWH seems, ironically, to hasten on the judgment. All this is somewhat reminiscent of Jeremiah, whose intercessions were also nipped in the bud, and whose opponents likewise expedited their own demise. There is a further analogy, in this connection, between the personal oracles of judgment against King Amaziah (Am. 7:17) and the prophet Hananiah (Je. 28:16).

Third, Amos knows a compulsion to prophesy (3:8b), shared with Jeremiah (20:9).

Amos is not alone in exhibiting features which are shared with *Jeremiah*. Micah does so too. Admittedly, certain features of Micah which have affinities with *Jeremiah* are perhaps somewhat closer to Isaiah, *e.g.* his treatment of the nations theme (1:2; 7:16–17). On the other hand, Micah shares the lawsuit-pattern (*rîb*, 6:1–5) with both *Jeremiah* and Hosea. He too knows an opposition which aims to silence him (2:6). And most interestingly, he exhibits at one point an involvement in his prophetic ministry which is not unlike that of Jeremiah in his Confessions.

The passage in question is 7:1–7. Specific echoes of *Jeremiah* abound in these verses: the self-apostrophe in verse 1, *cf.*

Jeremiah 15:10; the pictures of hunt and ambush in verse 2, *cf. Jeremiah* 12:6; 18:22–23; the radical social disintegration, by which the doing of evil has become a skill, and trust is impossible even within the closest relationships, in verses 3–6, *cf. Jeremiah* 9:1–8. The echoes of the last of these in particular have been widely observed, with some commentators taking the view that the Micah passage is dependent on *Jeremiah*. In reality, however, it is impossible to tell which way the influence has passed.[46]

The analogy with *Jeremiah* goes deeper, furthermore, for the passage is a lament of the prophet. It is not actually explicit who the speaker is. Some writers, observing that the speaker in verses 8–10 is apparently Zion (because both she and her enemy are feminine), have supposed that it is she who speaks also in verses 1–7. This is hard, however, to reconcile with the critique of the nation, from which the speaker seems to be apart, in verses 1, 7.

The role of verse 7 is important in the flow of the chapter. In the first instance, it should be read closely with the preceding verse, because of the adversative *wa'ᵃnî*, which corresponds to the first-person opening.[47] It can also be viewed, however, as transitional from the lament to the oracles that follow, which turn attention from judgment to salvation and vindication. Such a logic in itself would be at home in the lament, and here it is an appropriate means of bringing the whole prophecy to a climax. The transition, however, is thus not yet fully described, for it also provides the link between the prophet as speaker and Zion as speaker. Such an understanding does better justice to the relationship between the speakers in 1–7 and 8–10 than the view which simply equates them. The correspondence between prophet and nation which the relationship between the parts of verses 1–10 establishes is thus very similar to that which exists in *Jeremiah*.[48]

Micah 7:1–4 is one of the passages studied by N. Ittmann in his quest of prophetic texts which may provide a backcloth to Jeremiah's Confessions. It has in common with the Confessions not only the criticism of ungodliness, but also the sense of isolation which issues in an anticipation of judgment which reads, in the context, like a vindication of the prophet himself, verse 4b. Ittmann concludes that 7:1–4 stands in the Confessions *weite Vorfeld*. Hosea 9:14 stands in the same *Vorfeld*, the more so, in Ittmann's view, because Hosea turns disappointment about response to his message into prayer for judgment.[49] (Arguably, the prayer for judgment is also in Micah 7:4.) Ittmann concludes that neither Micah 7:1–4 nor Hosea 9:14 can be called a Confession, because they lack the decisive element of confrontation with YHWH, in which the lament becomes part of the message.[50]

In fact the Micah passage may stand even closer to the Confessions than Ittmann thinks. Micah 7:4b arguably shares with Hosea 9:14 the desire for judgment on the prophet's enemies. But more important is the analogy which we have already observed to exist between the voice in Micah 7:1–7 and that in 8–10. If, because of that juxtaposition, the sense of the 'indignation of the LORD' of verse 9 may be assumed to be part of the prophet's burden in 1–7, then the sentiment of those verses is close indeed to that of the Confessions, where Jeremiah protests to YHWH about the suffering he has to endure as a direct result of bearing his message to the people.

Even without this last observation, however, the importance of Ittmann's contribution should not be underestimated. It does much to show that the Confessions are a distinctively prophetic phenomenon, with antecedents in the prophetic literature. It is also significant that the two passages which stand closest to the Confessions are northern and southern respectively. Once again, therefore, there is evidence for a prophetic tradition which is defined not along regional lines but by a common stock of ideas on which both northern and southern prophets can draw.

Conclusions

We began our discussion of *Jeremiah*'s place within the Israelite prophetic tradition by observing similarities, stylistic and theological, between *Jeremiah* and Hosea. These turned especially on the theology of repentance found in both books. Each also had affinities with Deuteronomy 30:1–10, because of the belief in all three places in a return to the historical land as a result of a dramatic new redemptive act of YHWH.

We then considered how far *Jeremiah* might also have been influenced by other southern prophets. This was done by reference to recent studies of the prophets' role-labels and social locations, which tended to minimize differences between north and south. Furthermore, *Jeremiah* was seen to have a number of shared ideas and concerns with southern prophets, especially Amos and Micah. *Jeremiah* could be regarded as standing firmly within the Israelite prophetic tradition. The observations made bore upon the features of the book on a broad canvas, suggesting that, as on other occasions, it was not necessary to appeal to the Deuteronomist to account for them.

Conclusions

The foregoing study of *Jeremiah* raised in particular the question how far it could be regarded as the product of Deuteronomistic activity, according to the view that is held, in one form or another, by a large section of modern critical opinion about the book. One of our conclusions is in line with the 'Deuteronomistic' interpretation of *Jeremiah*, namely that the book is in some sense a 'redaction'. That is to say, individual units, which arose presumably in a variety of original settings, have been brought into the positions which they now occupy in the book in accordance with an over-arching concept which has shaped the whole. The material has a diversity which is consistent with its having been produced over a large time-span, yet also a unity which suggests an ordering of it according to a mature perspective. It follows that the development of the book was a complex process. We have not attempted to reconstruct that process, and have even expressed some scepticism about the possibility of the task, since the putative original units have so much been subordinated to the purposes of the final redaction.

To say so much, however, is by no means to agree that the book must have been produced either among Deuteronomistic circles or over a period spanning generations. *Jeremiah* does not have to be explained in terms either of Deuteronomistic programme, or of a profusion of fragments which recognizes no higher control. As regards affinities with the Deuteronomist, there are indeed similarities of style, and also of thought, between *Jeremiah*, Deuteronomy and DtH. To characterize *Jeremiah* as 'Deuteronomistic', however, was not meaningful, and could be sustained only by a kind of special pleading which redefined the term for application to the prophetic book. In part, this point was made by reference to long-recognized differences between the corpora (see further below); in part it depended on identifying a governing concept, which was distinct from that of DtH.

That concept had the theology of new covenant at its centre. The new covenant, however, was not the desperate last remedy of the disillusioned or the reactionary, nor a simple marker of Jeremiah's theological development. Rather, it governs the organization of all the material in a more or less thoroughgoing way. That is, it addresses essentially the question whether and how Israel may have a continued existence with YHWH, having exhibited, apparently definitively, her incapacity to be faithful to the covenant. This question underlies the organization of the mainly doom-laden, oracular material of chapters 1 – 24, the portrayal of the prophet in the so-called Confessions, the transition to a theology of hope in chapters 25 – 33 (36), and, in a particular way, the narrative of the last days of Judah and the aftermath of its fall (37 – 45).

To put the above point slightly differently, the issue which holds together this disparate material is the nature of the relationship between the divine and human action, as it bears upon the maintenance of the covenant and the people's destiny. Jeremiah's calls to repentance (chapter 3), standing at the beginning of the record of his exhortations, were presented in such a way as both to affirm the people's inability to respond, and to anticipate already the need for a redemptive act. The theme is then developed in the oracles of judgment generally (4 – 24). The Confessions too may be understood to contribute to the topic of divine and human action. This is because Jeremiah, as the one who hears and obeys the word of YHWH, in a sense substitutes for the people. Conversely, YHWH's relationship with Jeremiah testifies to his will to save the people in the end (*cf.* 15:19 and 31:18), and because Jeremiah also appears at times to suggest a kind of 'incarnation' of YHWH, the Confessions contain a hint of the involvement of YHWH himself in bringing it about.

YHWH's involvement in the ultimate salvation of the apostate people is the topic which is then developed in the chapters which contain the transition to a theology of hope. The 'Book of Consolation' (chapters 30 – 33, anticipated by 24:7) may be seen to address the question: how may a new act of redemption, conceived as an answer to the people's earlier persistent inability to maintain covenant faithfulness, both overcome the problem thus posed by the failure of the human will and preserve the reality of human responsibility? This is achieved in part by the theological statements of the 'Book of Consolation' itself (*e.g.* 31:31–34; 32:39–40), and in part by the structuring of the material on a broader canvas. That is, the 'Book of Consolation', with its declaration of a grand redemptive purpose of YHWH to which the people will give willing assent, leads into material which, first, emphasizes anew their stubbornness (34 – 36), then shows (with the vision of the basket of bad figs in mind, 24:8–10) that the judgment on those who went into Egypt, far from being the consequence of a kind of predestinarian *fiat*, was fully the result of the Palestinian remnant's choice. The oracles against the nations revive the theme of redemption, but nevertheless give way to a last word of caution, contained in the telling, once again, of the story of the fall of Judah.

The identification of a governing concept, which harnesses the diverse material of the book, also bears upon the question of its complexity as such. In this regard, our study was an attempt to follow a distinct methodological route from those which tend to characterize investigations of *Jeremiah*. Here too, our identification of a central intention of the redaction challenged the view that complexity in itself witnesses necessarily to a growth of the book over a time-span which must have exceeded that of the prophet's life, and to origins in many different times and places. To say this is not to deny the force of the basic observation about the diversity of the subject-matter, but to argue that it does not have its necessary consequence in the diverse authorship of the book.

175

With this issue in mind, we followed our study of the contents of *Jeremiah*, asking whether they were intelligible within the Israelite prophetic tradition. In the course of this study we argued for a basically unified prophetic tradition, in which north-south distinctions were not of decisive significance, and with which the main features of *Jeremiah* were consistent. The most important analogies between *Jeremiah* and earlier prophecy were with Hosea, which not only furnished a precedent for Jeremiah's preaching of repentance, but also anticipated the later book's theological reflection upon it. *Jeremiah* could not simply be placed within a so-called 'Ephraimite' tradition, however, without underestimating affinities which it had with the work of southern prophets also (Isaiah, Amos, Micah).

To place *Jeremiah* within a prophetic tradition was not thereby to minimize its dependence on Deuteronomy, despite the tendency of certain scholars to put Deuteronomy and prophecy in opposition to each other, and indeed our own insistence on the differences between *Jeremiah* and DtH. The relationship among the literary blocks in question (Deuteronomy, DtH, the prophetic tradition, *Jeremiah*) was in fact complex. *Jeremiah* and DtH could be shown to have reflected in their own distinct ways upon the theology of Deuteronomy, especially as contained in Deuteronomy 30:1–10. *Jeremiah*'s transition from judgment to hope (chapters 24, 25 – 33) can be shown to owe much to the promise of restoration of land in that passage, together with its insistence on the need for YHWH to act in a wholly new way with his people. At this point, dependence upon prophecy and dependence upon Deuteronomy are not in conflict, for Hosea's thought in this respect is also close to Deuteronomy. DtH, on the other hand (as represented by 1 Ki. 8:46–53), takes a consciously different route, in which the hope held out does not embrace restoration to the land. The judgment, therefore, that prophecy stands apart from Deuteronomy does not differentiate sufficiently between texts that are in some sense Deuteronomic. *Jeremiah*, in contrast, can be seen to depend both on earlier prophecy and on Deuteronomy.

Text-criticism and the prophet

To show that *Jeremiah* is fully intelligible within the Israelite prophetic tradition is not, admittedly, to prove that Jeremiah wrote the book. On the one hand, such a demonstration is probably, in the end, beyond the range of all historical investigation. On the other, the question raises additional issues to those we have addressed, notably the textual one.

It has not been part of the aim of this study to make an independent contribution to discussion of the textual issue in *Jeremiah*. I raise the matter here only to ask whether it might affect the conclusion, reached on the other grounds that have been outlined, that the subject-matter of the book could substantially be traced to the prophet. The answer, it seems to me, is that it does not.

A first reason for this judgment is drawn from text-critical studies proper. It is widely agreed today that LXX testifies to an underlying Hebrew text distinct from MT. The relationship between the two texts, therefore, cannot be described consistently in terms either of expansion of the one or of abbreviation of the other.[1] While the two texts may have influenced each other in the course of time, they represent essentially distinct text-types. Furthermore, the existence of these two text-types can be accounted for in terms of the bifurcation of an original common text which, according to Stulman,[2] must itself have been in existence for some time. Since, in his view, the divergence could have occurred as early as the end of the fifth century BC, the common text could go back to a period close to the prophet.

Secondly, the differences between MT and LXX are not congruent, or certainly not systematically so, with the differences which are frequently thought to exist between authentic Jeremianic material and the allegedly unauthentic. That is, all the different kinds of discourse found in MT are also found in LXX. Even where MT is held to have expansionist tendencies, testifying to a long period of development, this is not always thought to necessitate the conclusion that MT bears an inferior testimony to the life and work of the prophet. For example, E. Tov believes that *Jeremiah* 33:14–26, absent from LXX, may well be authentically Jeremianic, because it contains what he sees as typically Jeremianic expressions.[3] This example illustrates, furthermore, that the textual criticism of *Jeremiah* does not succeed in becoming an independent control in relation to literary criticism, wherein judgments concerning authenticity and secondariness diverge enormously.

Text-critical studies, therefore, would not appear to affect the conclusions reached otherwise in the present study in any way which would command agreement among scholars. Where LXX differs from MT on any text, whether it has featured in our argument or not, it does not follow that it has preserved the more ancient or authentic picture.[4]

The setting and purpose of *Jeremiah*

Our contention throughout has been that *Jeremiah* (MT) is a redaction which organized the oracles, speeches and narratives that compose it according to a governing concept and purpose. It remains to clarify that purpose, and ask what might have been the setting in which the book was finally produced.

The question must be answered first by reference to DtH. We noticed at the outset of our study certain important distinctions between the two corpora. Jeremiah nowhere gives clear support to the reform programme of Josiah; nor does he exhibit an attachment either to the monarchy or to the Jerusalem Temple, except in eschatological contexts which are not shared by DtH (such as 33:14–26). Conversely, Jeremiah is not mentioned by Kings in its account of the last days and fall of Judah, just where we might expect some allusion to the great prophet whose ministry focused precisely on those events.

Attempts have been made to understand the differences between the corpora in conventional literary- and historical-critical terms. It has been held, for example, that Jeremiah temporarily ceased to prophesy when Josiah carried out his reform, because he was basically in sympathy with it, and hoped that it would bring about the needed change of heart in Judah.[5] This argument is no longer persuasive, however, because it has been recognized that the reform probably began *before* Jeremiah's call, *i.e.* in 628 BC, as suggested by the account in 2 Chronicles 34 – 35.[6] In fact, it depended on the supposition that Jeremiah *must have been* in favour of the reform, because of certain ideas which he obviously shared with it. It did insufficient justice to the specific way in which those ideas were handled in *Jeremiah*. It could offer no explanation, furthermore, of Jeremiah's omission from Kings.

That omission, on the other hand, has been accounted for by Pohlmann on the hypothesis that the narrative in *Jeremiah* 40ff., which portrays Jeremiah's close involvement in events after the fall of Jerusalem, is largely imaginative, and that 2 Kings 25 represents an earlier and more reliable account. It is thus alleged that, in historical reality, Jeremiah was a less significant figure in the events surrounding the fall of Judah than the book of *Jeremiah* would have us think.[7] The theory is handicapped, however, by the need to suppose that, while *Jeremiah* 52 is substantially dependent on 2 Kings 25, 2 Kings 25:22–26 are an addition based on *Jeremiah* 40:7 – 43:7. The troublesome fact, therefore, that 2 Kings 25 has deliberately kept silent about Jeremiah is in the end inescapable, and even highlighted, though he did not intend it, by Pohlmann's analysis.

In reality, the differences between *Jeremiah* and DtH have to be explained on the broad canvas of the purposes of both corpora. First, their different approaches to Josiah's reform are, I believe, to be explained in terms of methodology. It was pointed out above (introduction) that the perceived problem arising from Jeremiah's coolness towards the reform rested on a misapprehension about the attitude of DtH to it. DtH, in its own way, showed that hopes reposed in the historic Davidic dynasty were doomed to disappointment.[8] The point has been reinforced by our interpretation of Jehoiakim's burning of the first scroll (*Jeremiah* 36), in relation to Josiah's reaction to the discovery of the 'book of the law' (2 Ki. 22).[9] DtH conveyed its attitude to the monarchy by means of a history of the kings, which showed the frustration of even their best efforts. Josiah's major role in Kings is essential to this concept. *Jeremiah*, however, chose a different method in pursuit of its intention to announce the demise of the historical monarchy, a method which depended on forthright condemnation. The faint praise reserved for Josiah in *Jeremiah* (22:15b–16) is to be understood in these terms. *Jeremiah*, furthermore, contains a promise of a wholly new kind of kingship, as part of its understanding of a new covenant between YHWH and a people reunited and restored to its ancient land (23:5f.; 33:14–26). In this, as we have seen, it is quite different from DtH, which offers no such hope. In *Jeremiah*, the hope of an eschatological kingly rule is another dimension of the difference in its presentation of the historical monarchy *vis-à-vis* DtH.

As for the omission of all reference to Jeremiah in DtH, the same sorts of considerations apply. Jeremiah is above all the prophet of the new covenant, the advocate of those very things which we have seen DtH refrains from holding out to his audience (especially in 1 Ki. 8:46–53). However we conceive of the relation between the two corpora in terms of precise setting, it is not surprising, perhaps, in view DtH's particular, restrained formulation of hope for the future of the exiles, that it should omit Jeremiah from its *dramatis personae*.

The aim of *Jeremiah*, finally, had two important dimensions. First, it explained and validated the judgment that had come in the form of the devastation of the land and the exile of its people. Second, it provided a credible basis for a future hope, in the face of the radical question which thus appeared to be put against the possible continuation of a covenant relationship between YHWH and his people. In articulating this theology of hope, however, the prophet was concerned not to allow the idea of redemption to overshadow the need for further covenant faithfulness. The picture he paints for the exiles is of a salvation made possible by a new redemptive act of YHWH, but characterized by a new capacity on their part to respond to him in truth.

To state the matter thus requires that the book, in broad substance, was brought into being in the exilic period, and (in accordance with our general hypothesis) in the lifetime of the prophet. It is impossible to be more precise. The final production did not, in any case, suddenly burst upon the scene. It was preceded, as the book itself suggests, by one, perhaps two, earlier scrolls containing words of the prophet. In addition, Jeremiah had already sent a letter, or letters, to the exiles, now contained in 29:4–28, soon after the first deportations to Babylon in 597 BC. The point is interesting, not only because it is in that context that Jeremiah first holds out to the exiles the hope of restoration to the land in due course (29:14), but also because it shows that he was concerned to communicate with them at a distance. The full story of the growth of the book is probably impossible to tell, as I have already argued. I would suggest, however, that it occurred in the context of the prophet's ongoing ministry, and in his latter years, possibly in the context of repeated communications with the exiles. Quite how, and whether, he could have continued to do this from Egypt is hard to know, as indeed is the bearing which this view of the growth of the book might have on the textual problem which we have discussed. The view which we have taken in this book, however, is that MT, or at least the substance of it, may be the latest stage in the prophet's own manifesto of hope for the exilic community.

181

Notes

Introduction

1 N. P. Lemche, *Ancient Israel: a New History of Israelite Society* (Sheffield, JSOT Press, 1988), pp. 44f.
2 R. P. Carroll, *Jeremiah* (Sheffield, JSOT Press, 1989), p. 55.
3 G. Garbini, *History and Ideology in Ancient Israel* (London, SCM, 1988), *e.g.* pp. 4–13.
4 Most recently in L. Stulman, *The Prose Sermons of the Book of Jeremiah* (Atlanta, Scholars Press, 1986), pp. 7–31.
5 B. Duhm, *Jeremia*, KHAT (Tübingen, Mohr, 1901), XI-XIII.
6 S. Mowinckel, *Zur Komposition des Buches Jeremia* (Kristiania, Jacob Dybwad, 1914), pp. 31ff.
7 E. W. Nicholson, *Preaching to the Exiles* (Oxford, Basil Blackwell, 1970), pp. 116ff.
8 E. Janssen, *Juda in der Exilszeit* (Göttingen, Vandenhoeck and Ruprecht, 1956).
9 J. P. Hyatt, 'The Deuteronomic Edition of Jeremiah', *VSH*, 1, 1951; 'The Book of Jeremiah', *IB*, 5, 1956, pp. 775–1142.
10 W. McKane, *Jeremiah 1–25*, I (Edinburgh, T. and T. Clark, 1986). The idea is expounded on pp. l-lxxxiii.
11 R. P. Carroll, *Jeremiah* (JSOT Press, 1989), pp. 65–82.
12 Th. Robinson, 'Baruch's Roll', *ZAW*, 42, 1924, pp. 209–221; O. Eissfeldt, *The Old Testament: An Introduction* (Oxford, Basil Blackwell, 1965), pp. 350–352.
13 J. Bright, 'The Date of the Prose Sermons of Jeremiah', *JBL*, 70, 1951, pp. 15–35.
14 H. Weippert, *Die Prosareden des Jeremiabuches* (Berlin, de Gruyter, 1973).
15 W. L. Holladay, *Jeremiah*, vol. II (Minneapolis, Augsburg/Fortress, 1989), p. 27.
16 *Ibid.*, pp. 78–80.
17 T. M. Raitt, *A Theology of Exile: Judgment/Deliverance in Jeremiah and Ezekiel* (Philadelphia, Fortress, 1977); J. Unterman, *From Repentance to Redemption: Jeremiah's Thought in Transition* (Sheffield, JSOT Press, 1987).

18 J. A. Thompson, *The Book of Jeremiah*, NICOT (Grand Rapids, Eerdmans, 1980).

19 R. R. Wilson, *Prophecy and Society in Ancient Israel* (Philadelphia, Fortress, 1980), and below, ch. 8, n.11.

20 L. Stulman, *Prose Sermons* (Scholars Press, 1986), pp. 12f. (citing Mowinckel, Rudolph, Hyatt).

21 E. Janssen, *Juda* (1956), pp. 105–108.

22 *E.g.* Colenso, as cited by S. R. Driver, *Deuteronomy*, ICC (Edinburgh, T. and T. Clark, 1895), p. xciv.

23 R. E. Friedman, *Who Wrote the Bible?* (Jonathan Cape, 1988), pp. 146–149, 208–210.

24 H. Weippert, *Prosareden* (Berlin, de Gruyter, 1973), pp. 22–24.

25 McKane, *Jeremiah 1–25* (1986), p. xlviii.

26 *Ibid.*, p. xlv.

27 Carroll, *Jeremiah* (1989), pp. 55–64, *cf.* p. 48.

28 See below, ch. 2.

29 Hyatt, 'Deuteronomic Edition', 1951, pp. 91ff.

30 *Cf.* Je. 11:4 with Dt. 4:20; 11:8a with Dt. 9:6; 11:8b with Dt. 27:15–26 (11:5 with Dt. 8:7–10).

31 *E.g.* (with respect to literary sophistication in DtH) R. Polzin, *Moses and the Deuteronomist* (New York, Seabury, 1980); B. Webb, *The Book of the Judges* (Sheffield, JSOT Press, 1987); H.-D. Hoffmann, *Reform und Reformen: Untersuchungen zu einem Grundthema in der deuteronomistischen Geschichtsschreibung* (Zürich, Theologischer Verlag, 1980); (with respect to a theology of grace) P. Diepold, *Israel's Land* (Stuttgart, Kohlhammer, 1972); J. G. McConville, *Law and Theology in Deuteronomy* (Sheffield, JSOT Press, 1984); (with respect to literary sophistication in Je.) T. Polk, *The Prophetic Persona* (Sheffield, JSOT Press, 1984).

32 Following the Chronicler's chronology of the events, 2 Ch. 34f.; on the likely plausibility of this, see E. W. Nicholson, *Deuteronomy and Tradition* (Oxford, Basil Blackwell, 1967), pp. 8–10, and further bibliography there.

33 See, *e.g.*, J. Skinner, *Prophecy and Religion* (Cambridge University Press, 1922), pp. 108–137.

34 *E.g.* Ho. 2:16f. (2:14f. EVV); 2:23–25 (2:21–23); 14:4–7.

35 Note especially the repeated use of the phrase *šûḇ šᵉḇûṭ* (to 'restore the fortunes', RSV); for references, see ch. 4, n. 9. *Cf.* Dt. 30:3; Ho. 6:11; and see below, ch. 8. On Jeremiah's preaching of repentance, see ch. 1.

36 F. M. Cross, *Canaanite Myth and Hebrew Epic* (Cambridge, Mass., Harvard University Press, 1973), pp. 274–289; R. D. Nelson, *The Double Redaction of the Deuteronomistic History* (Sheffield, JSOT Press, 1981).

37 G. von Rad, *Old Testament Theology*, I (Edinburgh and London, Oliver and Boyd, 1962), p. 343.

38 M. Noth, *The Deuteronomistic History* (Sheffield, JSOT Press, 1981); Hoffman, *Reform* (*passim*); T. R. Hobbs, *2 Kings* (Waco, Word, 1985), pp. xxivf.

39   J. G. McConville, 'Narrative and Meaning in the Books of Kings', *Biblica*, 70, 1989, pp. 31–49.
40   Below, ch. 2.
41   I have shown elsewhere that Solomon's prayer (especially 1 Ki. 8:46–53) seems consciously to distance itself from Dt. 30:1–10; J. G. McConville, 'I Kings viii 46–53 and the Deuteronomic Hope', *VT*, 42, 1992, pp. 67–79.
42   Nicholson, *Preaching* (1970), pp. 75ff.
43   Carroll, *Jeremiah* (1989), p. 42.
44   Numerous individual criticisms of the method have been made by J. Unterman, *From Repentance to Redemption: Jeremiah's Thought in Transition* (Sheffield, JSOT Press, 1987), *e.g.* pp. 27, 56f.
45   McKane, *Jeremiah 1–25* (1986), p. xlv.
46   See below, ch. 2.
47   See also K.-F. Pohlmann, *Studien zum Jeremiabuch: ein Beitrag zur Frage nach der Entstehung des Jeremiabuches* (Göttingen, Vandenhoeck and Ruprecht, 1978), who thinks that Je. 40ff. show a process of development *vis-à-vis* chs. 21, 24 towards the pro-Golah theology which he thinks now dominates the section; pp. 189f.
48   Polk's study of the 'persona' of Jeremiah is one which has emphasized the need for synchronic study, and which in the process has creatively interpreted a number of collocations which are often found difficult; his contributions are considered especially in ch. 3 below.
49   See discussion below, Conclusions.
50   Raitt, *Theology* (1977); Unterman, *Repentance* (1987); Holladay's idea of Jeremiah's development also seems to depend on a similar view, *Jeremiah* II (1989), pp. 25–35.
51   *E.g.* Unterman, *Repentance* (1987), 176f., 178; Unterman, however, does allow for some element of 'redaction', p. 178.

Chapter 1

1   J. A. Thompson, *The Book of Jeremiah* (Grand Rapids, Eerdmans, 1980), p. 167. *Cf.* Carroll, *Jeremiah* (JSOT Press, 1989), p. 122.
2   McKane, *Jeremiah 1–25* (1986), p. 31.
3   Holladay, *Jeremiah* I (1986), p. 85. For his general view of the composition of the chapter, see also pp. 62–68; and *cf.* pp. 23–25, 40, on 1:15.
4   See also N. Lohfink, 'Der junge Jeremia', in P.-M. Bogaert (ed.), *Jérémie*, pp. 351–368; *cf.* R. Albertz, 'Jer 2–6 und die Früzeitverkündigung Jeremias', *ZAW*, 94, 1982, pp. 20–47.
5   *E.g.* McKane, *Jeremiah 1–25* (1986), pp. 47f.
6   J. Bright, *Jeremiah*, AB (New York, Doubleday, 1965); Thompson, *Jeremiah* (1980); McKane, *Jeremiah* (1986).
7   W. L. Holladay, *Jeremiah*, vol. 1 (Philadelphia, Fortress, 1986), p. 54. Note, however, that he understands the verb to relate to Israel's sin, not her disgrace.

8   W. Rudolph, *Jeremia*, HAT (Tübingen, Mohr, 1947), p. 15; *cf.* p. 19.

9   Rudolph and others; *cf.* A. Weiser, *Das Buch des Propheten Jeremia*, ATD (Göttingen, Vandenhoeck and Ruprecht, 1969), NEB, see v. 16 as a reference to the future. It is quite possible, however, that a past reference is in mind here also, *e.g.* Hoshea's abortive quest for help from Pharaoh So, 2 Ki. 17:4. Some delete the verse as a late addition, which fits poorly. The interpretation offered here, however, makes a nice progression of thought from vv. 14–17 to v. 18.

10 Carroll, *Jeremiah* (1989), p. 129. *Cf.* Mark E. Biddle, *A Redaction History of Jeremiah 2:1–4:2* (Zürich, Theologischer Verlag, 1990), pp. 21–23. Contrast J. Milgrom, 'The Date of Jeremiah, Chapter 2', *JNES*, 14, 1955, pp. 65–69, who thought that 2:16, 36 must be dated to a time before the fall of Assyria, perhaps around 616 BC.

11 *Ibid.*

12 Holladay, *Jeremiah* I (1986), p. 96.

13 *Cf.* W. Rudolph, *Jeremia*, HAT (Mohr, 1947), p. 15; and see below, ch. 8.

14 Carroll, *Jeremiah* (1989), p. 129.

15 See n. 12.

16 Its originality in that place is sometimes disputed, as by Holladay, *Jeremiah* I (1986), p. 96. Yet there is no firm evidence for a gloss. It is not taken as such by all commentators on Daniel: see S. R. Driver, *Daniel* (Cambridge University Press, 1912), p. 153; J. Goldingay, *Daniel* (Dallas, Word, 1989), p. 275. Even if considered a gloss, it is most probably ancient; see Lacocque, *Daniel* (SPCK, 1979), p. 205.

17 In this I differ from Biddle, *Jeremiah* (1990). Biddle rightly opposes the view that Jeremiah actually preached repentance to the former northern kingdom. But I think he is wrong to deny that the idea of the north and its fate underlies the thought of Je. 2 and 3.

In Amos, 'Israel' probably connotes the northern kingdom at 5:1–3, 4, 25; 6:14; 7:10; it refers, on the other hand, to the historic people at 3:1f.; 7:8f., 15–17; see H. W. Wolff, *Joel and Amos* (Fortress, 1987), p. 164. Notice also the ironic use of the title 'King of Israel' in the Books of Kings, as if to draw attention to the discrepancy between the historic ideal and the divided reality; see McConville, 'Narrative', *Biblica*, 70, 1989, pp. 39–42.

18 McKane, *Jeremiah 1–25* (1986), p. 67.

19 Carroll, *Jeremiah* (1989), p. 145.

20 Rudolph, *Jeremiah* (1947), p. 23.

21 Bright, *Jeremiah* (1965), p. 26; Holladay, *Jeremiah* I (1986), p. 118, *cf.* pp. 62f.

22 Holladay, *ibid.*, p. 118.

23 Carroll, *Jeremiah* (1989), p. 145.

24 On these texts see further A. Schenker, 'Unwiderrufliche Umkehr und Neuer Bund. Vergleich zwischen der Wiederherstellung Israels in Dt. 4:25–31; 30:1–14 und dem neuen Bund in Jer. 31, 31–34', *FZPT*, 27, pp. 93–106.

Chapter 2

1   E. W. Nicholson, *Preaching to the Exiles* (Oxford, Basil Blackwell, 1970), pp. 12f. The problem is the emphasis on the Sabbath, which is not typical of Jeremiah. *Cf.* H. Weippert, *Prosareden* (Berlin, de Gruyter, 1973), p. 232, who acknowledges this difficulty.

2   *Cf.* T. W. Overholt, *The Threat of Falsehood* (SCM, 1970), for his comments on 9:1–5, see pp. 82f.

3   *E.g.* chs. 26 & 36; see Nicholson, *Preaching* (1970), pp. 106f.

4   See, *e.g.*, Bright, *Jeremiah* (1965), p. 56.

5   Gn. 22:18 is closer than Gn. 12:3 to the Je. passage, by virtue of the use of *brk* Hithpa., as opposed to Niph., and *gôy* as opposed to *mišpāḥâ*.

6   See further below on the oracles against the nations, ch. 7.

7   See, *e.g.*, 30:3, and below, ch. 7.

8   Overholt, 'The Falsehood of Idolatry: an Interpretation of Jeremiah x. 1–16', *JTS*, 16, 1965, pp. 1–12; Holladay, *Jeremiah* I (1986), p. 326.

9   Carroll, *Jeremiah* (1989), p. 254; *cf.* W. Thiel, *Die deuteronomistische Redaktion von Jeremia 1–25* (Neukirchen, Neukirchener Verlag, 1973), who does not treat the passage, regarding it as post-D., pp. 282, 288; B. N. Wambacq, 'Jérémie X, 1–16', *RB*, 81, 1974, pp. 57–62.

10   See below, ch. 4, *e.g.* on 30:12–17.

11   *E.g.* McKane, *Jeremiah 1–25* (1986), p. 169 (who also refers to Mowinckel, A. R. Johnson, H. G. Reventlow).

12   Carroll, *Jeremiah* (1989), pp. 212f., thinks the evidence is slender.

13   See, *e.g.*, C. Westermann, *Genesis 12–36* (SPCK, 1986), on 20:7; pp. 319f., 324.

14   The prohibition is virtually unique in the Old Testament, a fact which strengthens its cogency as an indicator of the redactional concerns of Je. 1–24. If there is an analogy with Ezekiel's dumbness (Ezk. 3:22–27, *cf.* 24:25–27; 33:21f.), as some have thought, it suggests that the prohibition is intended only to have a temporary effect in Je.; R. R. Wilson, 'An Interpretation of Ezekiel's Dumbness', *VT*, 22, 1972, pp. 91–104; Holladay, *Jeremiah* I (1986), p. 253.

15   Thiel, *Redaktion 1–25* (1973), pp. 210–218; Carroll, *Jeremiah* (1989), p. 371; McKane, *Jeremiah 1–25* (1986), p. 424f.

16   Carroll, *Jeremiah* (1989), p. 372.

17   McKane, *Jeremiah 1–25* (1986), p. 425.

18   Carroll, *Jeremiah* (1989), p. 373.

19   McKane, *Jeremiah 1–25* (1986), p. 426. In this he resembles Nicholson, *Preaching* (1970), pp. 25ff. *Cf.* above, Introduction.

20   Thiel, *Redaktion 1–25* (1973), p. 210; Weippert, *Prosareden* (1973), pp. 55–57; McKane, *Jeremiah 1–25* (1986), p. 426.

21   Carroll, *Jeremiah* (1989), 406f.

22   See remarks above, Introduction; and *cf.* below, Conclusions, on the same topic.

23   *Cf.* von Rad, *OT Theology I*, p. 343, on 2 Ki. 25:27–30; and contrast M. Noth, *Deuteronomistic History* (JSOT, 1981), pp. 12, 98. Here again, our

interest in the context of statements in the whole book affects our interpretation. But see Conclusions.

24 Nicholson, *Preaching* (1970), 42f.
25 On the meaning of Jehoiakim's action, see Holladay, *Jeremiah* II (1989), pp. 259f.
26 See above, Introduction, nn. 38, 39, to Hoffmann, Hobbs, McConville.
27 See also Pohlmann, *Studien* (1978), pp. 19f., 31, who thinks Je. 24 is from the same author as 37 – 44 in its present form, and that the latter narrative was written in favour of a pro-Golah interpretation of Jeremiah's preaching; *cf.* Nicholson, *Preaching* (1970), pp. 110f. We shall return to this theory below (ch. 5).

Chapter 3

1 *Cf.*, *e.g.*, Pss. 46, 121; Is. 31:4f.; 43:1–7.
2 See T. W. Overholt, *Falsehood* (SCM, 1970), pp. 24–48.
3 For a delimitation of the Confessions, see G. von Rad, *OT Theology* II (Edinburgh, Oliver and Boyd, 1965), p. 201 n.
4 J. S. Skinner, *Prophecy* (Cambridge University Press, 1922), p. 201, citing J. Wellhausen, *Israelitische und Jüdische Geschichte*[5], p. 149. See also above on Duhm, Introduction (n. 5).
5 For actual parallels, see W. Baumgartner, *Jeremiah's Poems of Lament* (Sheffield, Almond, 1988), pp. 41ff., 79ff.; and *cf.* Carroll, *From Chaos to Covenant* (SCM, 1981), pp. 107ff.
6 Baumgartner, *Poems* (1988), p. 16; see other bibliography there. For an account of the rise of 'Individualism' in Israel, see H. W. Robinson, *The Religious Ideas of the Old Testament* (Duckworth, 1913), pp. 87–91.
7 *Ibid.*, p. 45.
8 *Ibid.*, pp. 98f.
9 C. Westermann, *Basic Forms of Prophetic Speech* (Lutterworth, 1967), especially pp. 169ff.
10 H. G. Reventlow, *Liturgie und Prophetisches Ich bei Jeremia* (Gütersloh, Mohn, 1963), pp. 7–11.
11 *Ibid.*, pp. 12f.
12 U. Mauser, *Gottesbild und Menschwerdung* (Tübingen, Mohr, 1971), p. 53.
13 *Ibid.*, pp. 55f.
14 *Ibid.*, pp. 58f.
15 *Ibid.*, p. 78.
16 *Ibid.*, p. 82. In this regard, he appeals to von Rad.
17 *E.g.* Bright, *Jeremiah* (1965), p. 67; Rudolph, *Jeremia* (1947), p. 56.
18 Polk, *Persona* (1984), p. 80.
19 *Ibid.*, pp. 82–102.
20 *Ibid.*, p. 83.
21 *Ibid.*, pp. 87ff.

22 *Ibid.*, pp. 93–102.
23 *Ibid.*, pp. 87f.
24 F. D. Hubmann, *Untersuchungen zu den Konfessionen Jer 11:8–12:6 und 15:10–21* (Würzburg, Echter Verlag, 1978); N. Ittmann, *Die Konfessionen Jeremias* (Neukirchen, Neukirchener Verlag, 1981); A. R. Diamond, *The Confessions of Jeremiah in Context* (Sheffield, JSOT Press, 1987); K. O'Connor, *The Confessions of Jeremiah: their Interpretation and Role in Chapters 1–25* (Atlanta, Scholars Press, 1988); M. S. Smith, *The Laments of Jeremiah and their Contexts* (Atlanta, Scholars Press, 1990).
25 Hubmann, Ittmann, Diamond, *ibid.*, Polk, *Persona* (1984).
26 Ittmann, *Konfessionen* (1981), pp. 34f., 71f., 79.
27 *Ibid.*, p. 68. He also notices that the portrayal of enemies is always in prose, thus recognizing the limits of the prose-poetry criterion of authenticity; p. 69.
28 *Ibid.*, p. 78.
29 Diamond, *Confessions* (1987), pp. 135–146.
30 *Ibid.*, p. 157.
31 *Ibid.*, pp. 169, 183.
32 *Ibid.*, p. 163.
33 *Ibid.*, p. 162.
34 Polk, *Persona* (1984), p. 101.
35 *Ibid.*, p. 102.
36 Ittmann, *Konfessionen* (1981), p. 26.
37 See, *e.g.*, Diamond, *Confessions* (1987), pp. 142–144.
38 Ittmann, *Konfessionen* (1981), p. 19; *cf.* von Rad, *OT Theology II* (1965), pp. 203f.
39 W. L. Holladay, *The Architecture of Jeremiah 1–20* (Associated University Presses, 1976), p. 18.
40 D. J. A. Clines and D. M. Gunn, 'Form, Occasion and Redaction in Jeremiah 20', *ZAW*, 88, 1976, p. 408.
41 For the 'certainty of a hearing' as an element in the individual laments, see W. H. Bellinger, *Psalmody and Prophecy* (Sheffield, JSOT Press, 1984), pp. 23f. (78–82); Baumgartner, *Poems* (1988), pp. 35f.; C. Westermann, *Praise and Lament in the Psalms* (Edinburgh, T. and T. Clark, 1981), pp. 64–70.
42 Clines and Gunn, 'Form', *ZAW*, 88, 1976, p. 408.
43 See further below, ch. 4.
44 Carroll, *Chaos* (SCM, 1981), pp. 111f.
45 McKane, *Jeremiah 1–25* (1986), p. xciv.
46 *Ibid.*
47 *Ibid.*, p. xcvi.
48 *Cf.* Diamond, *Confessions* (1987), p. 123 (though he ultimately seems undecided about the extent of Deuteronomistic influence in the editing of Je. 11–20; *cf.* pp. 188, 190).

Chapter 4

1   The place of Je. 25 in the structure of the book is complicated, of
    course, by the question of the original place of the oracles against the
    nations (chs. 46 – 51, MT, but placed after 25:13 in LXX). See the
    treatment of these below (ch. 7) for my view that the MT's order may
    well be original.
2   Holladay, *Jeremiah* II (1989), pp. 23f. *Cf.* K. O'Connor, '"Do not Trim
    a Word": the Contribution of Chapter 26 to the Book of Jeremiah',
    CBQ, 51, 1989, p. 618.
3   *E.g.* C. R. Seitz, 'The Prophet Moses and the Canonical Shape of
    Jeremiah', *ZAW*, 101, 1989, p. 12. M. Kessler, 'Jeremiah Chapters 26
    – 45 Reconsidered', *JNES*, 27, 1968, pp. 81–88, is ambivalent on the
    point.
4   Pohlmann observes that there is general agreement on the unity of
    the section, though disagreement as to whether it is the result of
    substantial redactional activity; *Studien* (1978), p. 49. G. Wanke, *Unter-
    suchungen zur sogenannten Baruchschrift* (Berlin, de Gruyter, 1971),
    finds a considerable amount of such activity, and he has been largely
    followed by Holladay, *Jeremiah* II, p. 13. Rudolph and Weiser, on the
    other hand, found less.
5   Nicholson, *Preaching* (1970), pp. 16f.; O'Connor, 'Trim', pp. 625f.;
    Holladay, *Jeremiah* II, p. 23.
6   J. Applegate, *Structure and Theology in Jeremiah 32:1–34:7: Hope for
    Judah and the Fate of Zedekiah*, PhD thesis (Trinity College, Bristol,
    1985), pp. 239–248.
7   See our remarks above on 1 Ki. 8:46–53 (Introduction).
8   See above, Introduction.
9   *Viz.* 29:14; 30:3, 18; 31:23; 32:44; 33:7, 11, 26; 48:47; 49:6, 39.
10 Thompson, *Jeremiah*, p. 511; *cf.* Weiser, *Jeremiah*, p. 216.
11 See Mauser on the idea of a time of wrath; i.e. wrath is not God's
    unchanging attitude, but his attitude now; *Gottesbild*, p. 93.
12 Nicholson, *Preaching* (1970); *cf.* n. 5.
13 Je. 7:1–15 and 26:2–6 are often simply seen as two different accounts
    of the same sermon; *e.g.* Skinner, *Prophecy*, pp. 170f.; Thompson,
    Jeremiah, p. 273. McKane thinks arguments about the priority of
    either passage are unsatisfactory; *Jeremiah 1–25*, p. 158f. Thiel
    believes the oldest kernel in either is 7:14, but that both have been
    heavily worked over by 'D', *Redaktion 1–25*, p. 105. Some, however,
    see 7:1–15 as prior, regarding the briefer passage as resumptive in
    character; *e.g.* Weippert, *Prosareden*, pp. 29–32.
14 *Cf.* Carroll, *Jeremiah*, pp. 516f.; O'Connor, 'Trim', pp. 62f.
15 Contrast McKane's belief that Jeremiah could not have portrayed
    himself as a salvation-prophet; *Jeremiah 1–25*, p. xciv. See also B. S.
    Childs' treatment of the passage, *Old Testament Theology in a Canonical
    Context* (Philadelphia, Fortress, 1985), pp. 135–139.
16 Mowinckel, *Zur Komposition* (1914), pp. 45–47.

17 See above, ch. 1.
18 Chs. 32f. are commonly regarded as a secondary expansion to 31f.;
    see, *e.g.*, Carroll, *Jeremiah*, pp. 625, 634.
19 See G. von Rad, *Genesis* (SCM, 1961), pp. 122f.
20 See R. W. L. Moberly, *At the Mountain of God* (Sheffield, JSOT Press,
    1983), pp. 88–91. (Moberly points out the parallels between the Gen-
    esis and Exodus passages.)
21 Carroll regards it as impossible that Jeremiah could have made such a
    volte-face as to utter these prophecies, and prefers to attribute 30f. to
    circles during and after the exile that derived from the *shalom*-
    prophets; *Jeremiah*, p. 569. He does, however, distinguish the hope
    here from D. It is rather *post*-D., though connected with Dt. 30:1–10.
22 Von Rad, *OT Theology II*, pp. 212–217; Bright, *Jeremiah*, p. 287; Hyatt,
    Jeremiah, p. 1037.
23 Duhm, *Jeremiah*, pp. 255–258; Carroll, *Chaos*, pp. 217–223; *cf. idem*,
    Jeremiah, pp. 611f.
24 On the integrity of 33:14–26 within the chapter, see the discussion
    below of the relationship between MT and LXX (Conclusions).
25 See R. Polzin, *Moses*, pp. 49–52.
26 *Pace* Carroll, *Jeremiah*, pp. 611–614.
27 See above, n. 5.
28 *Cf.* Hoffmann, on the positive character of a death followed by a
    decent burial, *Reform*, pp. 181–187.

Chapter 5

1 Wanke, *Baruchschrift* (1971), pp. 91–132.
2 Our treatment is closer in this respect to Pohlmann, *Studien* (1978).
3 Regarding the structure of (24)25 – 45, Pohlmann's view is somewhat
   similar. He sees 24 as a preface to 25 – 45, within which, first, its
   theology of salvation is elaborated (chs. 25 – 36, especially 27 – 33),
   then its view of the fate of the group (corresponding to the basket of
   'bad figs') to which salvation was not offered (chs. 37 – 45); *Studien*,
   p. 46.
4 Approximately with Kessler, 'Jeremiah 26–45', pp. 84f. See also Wanke's more elaborate division of 37:11 – 43:7, in which the recurring
   phrase *wayyēšeḇ yirmᵉyāhû* plays a structuring role; *Baruchschrift*, p. 93.
5 See Wanke, *ibid.*, p. 151.
6 *E.g.* Pohlmann on 38:1–6, 7–13; *Studien*, pp. 76, 83. *Cf.* Applegate's
   idea of a debate within the redaction of Je., *Structure*, pp. 315–321; his
   discussion effectively highlights the tensions within the Zedekiah
   material.
7 See M. Greenberg, *Ezekiel 1–20*, AB (New York, Doubleday, 1983).
8 On the basis of this antithesis Pohlmann regards 24:7 as overloaded,
   Studien, pp. 23f. The same antithesis underlies Unterman's thesis. See
   his review of the literature on the relationship between repentance-

and redemption-theologies, with special reference to 24:7 and 31:31–34; *Repentance*, pp. 13–16.

9   Pohlmann, *Studien*, pp. 123–145, especially pp. 136–138.
10 See McConville, 'Narrative', p. 48.
11 *E.g.* Bright, *Jeremiah*, pp. 185f.
12 See above, ch. 4.
13 Wanke, *Baruchschrift* (1971), p. 152.
14 Kessler, 'Jeremiah 26–45' (1968), p. 86.
15 Wanke, *Baruchschrift* (1971), p. 152.

Chapter 6

1 See above, ch. 5. The treatment of the role of the prophet in 37 – 45 offered here contrasts with Wanke's view that it consists merely in portraying the rejection of the world by the people.
2 See above, ch. 3.
3 Ch. 5.
4 See discussion above, ch. 4 (and n. 14).
5 Holladay, *Jeremiah* I (1986), p. 574; Thompson, *Jeremiah* (1980), p. 469.

Chapter 7

1   Duhm, *Jeremiah* (1901), pp. 336f.
2   See D. L. Christensen, *Transformations of the War Oracle in Old Testament Prophecy* (Missoula, Scholars Press, 1975), pp. 3f., referring to A. Bentzen, 'The Ritual Background of Amos i 2 – ii 16', *OTS* 8, 1950, pp. 85–99, and H. G. Reventlow, *Das Amt des Propheten bei Amos* (Göttingen, Vandenhoeck and Ruprecht, 1980).
3   Mendenhall's work on ANE treaties [*Law and Covenant in the Ancient Near East* (Pittsburgh, Biblical Colloquium, 1955)] influenced Reventlow in this respect; see D. L. Christensen, *op. cit.*, p. 4.
4   N. K. Gottwald, *All the Kingdoms of the Earth* (New York, Harper and Row, 1964), p. 49.
5   Rudolph, *Jeremia*, pp. 228–230.
6   Wolff, *Joel and Amos*, pp. 141f., 147f.
7   See Holladay, *Jeremiah* II, pp. 402ff.
8   J. H. Hayes, 'The Usage of Oracles against foreign Nations in Ancient Israel', *JBL*, 87, 1968, pp. 81–92.
9   Christensen, *Transformations* (1975), see *e.g.* pp. 281ff.
10 Thiel, *Redaktion 1–25*, p. 281.
11 Carroll, *Jeremiah*, p. 753.
12 Christensen, *Transformations*, pp. 262f.; Holladay, *Jeremiah* II, pp. 401–415.
13 Rudolph, *Jeremia*, p. 256.
14 Carroll, *Jeremiah*, p. 753.

15 Ibid., p. 758; *cf.* Rudolph, pp. 250f.; Duhm, p. 355; Holladay, *Jeremiah* II, p. 371.
16 Carroll, *ibid.*, pp. 755f.
17 *Ibid.*, p. 753.
18 *Ibid.*, p. 496.
19 Christensen, *Transformations* (1975), pp. 262f.
20 Carroll, *Jeremiah*, p. 753, *cf.* p. 759; *cf.* again Rudolph, p. 256.
21 See above, ch. 4.
22 Duhm, *Jeremiah* (1901), p. 355.
23 *Cf.* C. F. Keil, *Jeremiah and Lamentations* (Grand Rapids, Eerdmans, 1973), p. 244: '. . . those who should not be compelled to drink'; and S. R. Driver, *Jeremiah* (Hodder and Stoughton, 1906), p. 294: '. . . they to whom it pertained not to drink the cup'. He elucidates *'mishpat'* as 'judgment (or sentence, or right)'.
24 Above, ch. 4.
25 K. T. Aitken, 'The Oracles against Babylon in Jeremiah 50–51: Structures and Perspectives', *TynB* 35, 1984, pp. 25–63; see pp. 25f. and nn. for an account of views taken of the composition of Je. 50f., ranging from four separate compositions (Condamin) to fifty (T. H. Robinson)!
26 *Ibid.*, p. 26.
27 *Ibid.*, p. 28.
28 *Ibid.*, pp. 31–33.
29 Christensen, *Transformations*, p. 260.
30 This connection is noted by Holladay, *Jeremiah* II, p. 415.
31 Above, ch. 4.
32 Aitken, 'Oracle', 1984, p. 57.
33 *e.g.* Rudolph, Holladay.
34 Holladay, *Jeremiah* II (1989), p. 389.
35 Rudolph, *Jeremia* (1947), *e.g.* pp. 249, 255.
36 Carroll, *Jeremiah*, pp. 755f.
37 See above, ch. 2.
38 Ch. 4, n. 9.
39 Carroll, *Jeremiah*, p. 756.
40 Holladay's interpretation of the oracles against the nations is broadly consistent with that offered here, because of the parallels he sees between them and the 'Book of Consolation' (Je. 30 – 33); *Jeremiah* II, pp. 414f.; *cf.* Seitz, 'Prophet Moses', pp. 24f.

Chapter 8

1 Wilson, *Prophecy* (Fortress, 1980), pp. 135–252.
2 *E.g.* M. Weinfeld, *Deuteronomy and the Deuteronomic School* (Oxford, Clarendon, 1972), pp. 366–370.
3 Von Rad, *Studies*, pp. 61f., 69; *cf. OT Theology I*, p. 220; *Deuteronomy*, pp. 12–15.

4   J. Muilenburg, 'The "Office" of the Prophet in Ancient Israel', in J. P. Hyatt (ed.), *The Bible in Modern Scholarship* (Abingdon, 1965), pp. 74–97; H.-J. Kraus, *Worship in Israel: a Cultic History of the Old Testament* (Oxford, Basil Blackwell, 1966), pp. 101–112.

5   Muilenburg, *ibid.*, especially pp. 78–89, 96.

6   See R. E. Clements, 'Pentateuchal Problems', in G. W. Anderson (ed.), *Tradition and Interpretation* (Oxford, Clarendon, 1979), p. 100; referring to S. Mowinckel, *Erwägungen zur Pentateuchquellenfrage* (Oslo, 1964), pp. 59–118. *Cf.* G. J. Wenham, *Genesis 1–15* (Waco, Word, 1987), p. xxx. Note in this connection the tendency to question the four-source theory altogether; *e.g.* R. Rendtorff, *The Problem of the Process of Transmission of the Pentateuch* (Sheffield, JSOT Press, 1990).

7   Clements, 'Problems', pp. 99–101.

8   J. Weiser, *Introduction to the Old Testament* (DLT, 1961), pp. 115–121.

9   *Ibid.*, p. 118.

10 Clements, 'Problems', pp. 120–122.

11 Wilson, *Prophecy*; see, *e.g.*, pp. 144, 146; *cf.* Brekelmans, *SVT*, 15, 1966, pp. 90–96.

12 J. L. Kugel, *The Idea of Biblical Poetry* (New Haven, Yale University Press, 1981), p. 83 (on 'rhythmical prose'); p. 85 (on a 'continuum' from poetry to prose); pp. 87–92 (on the special features that mark poetry).

13 F. I. Andersen-D. N. Freedman, *Hosea*, AB (New York, Doubleday, 1980), p. 60.

14 *Ibid.*, pp. 57–59.

15 H. W. Wolff, *Hosea* (Philadelphia, Fortress, 1974), pp. 57f.; J. L. Mays, *Hosea* (SCM, 1969), p. 54; Andersen-Freedman, *Hosea*, p. 292.

16 Westermann, *Basic Forms*, p. 207.

17 Thiel, *Redaktion 1–25*, p. 108 (*i.e.* his belief that 7:3, while using similar language to the 'authentic' 2:33, contradicts it, and cannot be from Jeremiah, since Jeremiah did not believe that Israel could 'do good').

18 H. Weippert, 'Der Beitrag ausserbiblischer Prophetentexte zum Verständnis der Prosareden des Jeremiabuches', in P. M. Bogaert (ed.), *Jérémie*, pp. 83–104, opposes Thiel's view that the warning element in the sermons is a post-eventum reflection on the events of 587 BC, p. 91; on the treaty-background to prophecy, pp. 93–97.

19 Wolff, *Hosea*, pp. 108f.; Mays, *Hosea*, pp. 93f.

20 Wolff, *ibid.*, p. 214.

21 G. I. Emmerson, *Hosea: an Israelite Prophet in Judean Perspective* (Sheffield, JSOT Press, 1984), p. 48.

22 See Wolff's note to Procksch, Budde, *Hosea*, p. 25, n. 4.

23 *Ibid.*, pp. 25f.

24 *Ibid.*, p. 47.

25 *Ibid.*, p. 59.

26 *Ibid.*, p. 196.

27 Weippert, *Prosareden* (1973), *e.g.* p. 43, on Je. 12 – an ironic use of a D.

phrase? *Cf.* p. 81, where she minimizes the dependence of the Temple sermon on Dt.

28 Carroll, *Jeremiah*, p. 72.
29 Muilenburg, 'Office', p. 95.
30 Wilson, *Prophecy* (1980), pp. 260f.
31 *Ibid.*, p. 254.
32 D. L. Petersen, *The Roles of Israel's Prophets* (Sheffield, JSOT Press, 1981), pp. 35ff.
33 *E.g.* H. Fuhs, *Sehen und Schauen: die Wurzel ḥzh im alten Orient und im alten Testament* (Würzburg, Echter Verlag, 1978); Petersen, *ibid.*, p. 52.
34 D. L. Petersen, *The Roles of Israel's Prophets* (Sheffield, JSOT Press, 1981), p. 63.
35 *Ibid.*, p. 54.
36 *Ibid.*, pp. 57f.
37 *Ibid.*, p. 57.
38 *Ibid.*, pp. 60f.
39 *Ibid.*, p. 60.
40 *Ibid.*, p. 62.
41 Against Petersen, *ibid.*, p. 59. By the same token, *ḥōzeh* would have to be suspect at Mi. 3:7; *cf.* Wilson, *Prophecy* (1980), p. 256.
42 Wilson, *ibid.*
43 Petersen, *Roles* (1981), pp. 87f.
44 *Ibid.*, pp. 35ff.
45 *Ibid.*, p. 60.
46 D. R. Hillers, *Micah* (Fortress, Philadelphia, 1984), p. 85 – despite the presence of the noun *ḥāsîd*, v. 2.
47 *Ibid.*
48 *Cf. e.g.* our treatment above of Je. 14–15, with its interplay between prophet and nation (ch. 3); similar transitions to that which we have found here also occur in Je. to suggest the nature of the relationship between Jeremiah and YHWH; *e.g.* Je. 8:22 – 9:5; see again ch. 3, above.
49 Ittmann, *Konfessionen* (1981), pp. 32–34; note also Wolff, *Hosea* (1974), p. 163: '. . . our passage is one of the historical antecedents of Jeremiah's Confessions, particularly those Confessions which are combined with a divine oracle'.
50 Ittmann, *ibid.*, pp. 34f.

Conclusions

1 J. G. Janzen, *Studies in the Text of Jeremiah* (Cambridge, Mass., Harvard University Press, 1973), pp. 1–8 (for a history of discussion); pp. 87–114 (on supposed abridgement in LXX); *cf.* McKane, *Jeremiah 1–25*, p. xvii.
2 L. Stulman, *Prose Sermons*, p. 2; *cf.* Janzen, *ibid.*, pp. 131f. – for his view that no substantial block of material requires a post-exilic date.

3   E. Tov, 'Some Aspects of the Textual and Literary History of the Book of Jeremiah', in P. M. Bogaert (ed.), *Le Livre de Jérémie*, p. 154. Holladay, however, disagrees, *Jeremiah* II, pp. 8, 228–232.
4   *E.g.* Holladay, *Jeremiah* II, pp. 6f.; and *cf.* A. R. Diamond, 'Jeremiah's Confessions in the LXX and MT: a witness to developing canonical function?', *VT*, 40, 1990, pp. 33–50, who argues that LXX is closer than MT in the Confessions to generic lament.
5   See Skinner, *Prophecy* (1922), pp. 108f.; his own position, pp. 109ff., is more subtle.
6   Nicholson, *Deuteronomy* (1967), pp. 7–13.
7   Pohlmann, 'Erwägungen', in *Textgemäss* (1979), pp. 96–99.
8   Above, Introduction; and McConville, 'Narrative', *Biblica*, 70, 1989.
9   Above, ch. 2.

Bibliography

Ackroyd, P. R., *Exile and Restoration* (SCM, 1968).

Ackroyd, P. R., 'The Book of Jeremiah – Some Recent Studies', *JSOT*, 28, 1984, pp. 47–59.

Aitken, K. T., 'The Oracles Against Babylon in Jeremiah 50–51: Structures and Perspectives', *TynB* 35, 1984, pp. 25–63.

Albertz, R., 'Jer 2–6 und die Frühzeitverkündigung Jeremias', *ZAW*, 94, 1982, pp. 20–47.

Andersen, F. I. and Freedman, D. N., *Hosea*, AB (New York, Doubleday, 1980).

Applegate, J., *Structure and Theology in Jeremiah 32:1 – 34:7: Hope for Judah and the Fate of Zedekiah*, unpublished PhD thesis (Trinity College, Bristol, 1985).

Auld, A. G., 'Prophets and Prophecy in Jeremiah and Kings', *ZAW*, 96, 1984, pp. 86–82.

Baumgartner, W., *Jeremiah's Poems of Lament* (Sheffield, Almond, 1988).

Begrich, J., 'Das priesterliche Heilsorakel', *ZAW*, 52, 1934, pp. 81–92.

Bellinger, W. H., *Psalmody and Prophecy* (Sheffield, JSOT Press, 1984).

Bentzen, A., 'The Ritual Background of Amos i 2 – ii 16', *OTS*, 8, 1950, pp. 85–99.

Berridge, J. M., *Prophet, People and the Word of Yahweh* (Zürich, EVZ, 1970).

Biddle, Mark E., *A Redaction History of Jeremiah 2:1 – 4:2*, AThANT 77 (Zürich, Theologischer Verlag, 1990).

Blenkinsopp, J., *A History of Prophecy in Israel: from the Settlement in the Land to the Hellenistic Period* (Philadelphia, Westminster, 1983).

Bogaert, P. M. (ed.), *Le Livre de Jérémie: Le Prophète et son Milieu, les Oracles et leur Transmission* (Leuven University Press, 1981).

Bright, J., 'The Date of the Prose Sermons of Jeremiah', *JBL*, 70, 1951, pp. 15–35.

Bright, J., *Jeremiah*, AB (New York, Doubleday, 1965).

Carroll, R. P., *From Chaos to Covenant* (SCM, 1981).

Carroll, R. P., *Jeremiah*, OTL (SCM, 1986).

Carroll, R. P., *Jeremiah* (Sheffield, JSOT Press, 1989).

Carroll, R. P., 'Radical Clashes of Will and Style: Recent Commentary Writing on the Book of Jeremiah', *JSOT*, 45, 1989, pp. 99–114.

Childs, B. S., *Old Testament Theology in a Canonical Context* (Philadelphia, Fortress, 1985).

Christensen, D. L., *Transformations of the War Oracle in Old Testament Prophecy* (Missoula, Scholars Press, 1975).

Clements, R. E., *God and Temple* (Oxford, Basil Blackwell, 1965).

Clements, R. E., 'Pentateuchal Problems', in G. W. Anderson (ed.), *Tradition and Interpretation* (Oxford, Clarendon, 1979), pp. 96–124.

Clements, R. E., *Prophecy and Tradition* (Oxford, Basil Blackwell, 1975).

Clines, D. J. A. and Gunn, D. M., 'Form, Occasion and Redaction in Jeremiah 20', *ZAW*, 88, 1976, pp. 390–409.

Craigie, P. C., Kelley, Page H. and Drinkard, Joel F., *Jeremiah 1–25* (Dallas, Word, 1991).

Cross, F. M., *Canaanite Myth and Hebrew Epic* (Cambridge, Mass., Harvard University Press, 1973).

Diamond, A. R., 'Jeremiah's Confessions in the LXX and MT: a witness to developing canonical function?', *VT*, 40, 1990, pp. 33–50.

Diamond, A. R., *The Confessions of Jeremiah in Context* (Sheffield, JSOT Press, 1987).

Diepold, P., *Israel's Land*, BWANT 95 (Stuttgart, Kohlhammer, 1972).

Duhm, B., *Jeremia*, KHAT (Tübingen, Mohr, 1901).

Driver, S. R., *Daniel* (Cambridge, Cambridge University Press, 1912).

Driver, S. R., *Deuteronomy*, ICC (Edinburgh, T. and T. Clark, 1895).

Driver, S. R., *Jeremiah* (Hodder and Stoughton, 1906).

Eissfeldt, O., *The Old Testament: an Introduction* (Oxford, Basil Blackwell, 1965).

Emmerson, G. I., *Hosea: An Israelite Prophet in Judean Perspective* (Sheffield, JSOT Press, 1984).

R. E. Friedman, *Who Wrote the Bible?* (Jonathan Cape, 1988).

Fuhs, H., *Sehen und Schauen: Die Wurzel ḥzh im Alten Orient und im Alten Testament. Ein Beitrag zum prophetischen Offenbarungsempfang*, FB 32 (Würzburg, Echter, 1978).

Garbini, G., *History and Ideology in Ancient Israel* (SCM, 1988).

Goldingay, J., *Daniel* (Dallas, Word, 1989).

Gottwald, N. K., *All the Kingdoms of the Earth: Israelite Prophecy and International Relations in the Ancient Near East* (New York, Harper and Row, 1964).

Greenberg, M., *Ezekiel 1–20*, AB (New York, Doubleday, 1983).

Gunneweg, A. H. J., 'Konfession oder Interpretation im Jeremiabuch', *ZTK*, 67, 1970, pp. 395–416.

Habel, N., 'The Form and Significance of the Call Narratives', *ZAW*, 77, 1965, pp. 297–323.

Hayes, J. H., 'The Usage of Oracles Against Foreign Nations in Ancient Israel', *JBL*, 87, 1968, pp. 81–92.

Heschel, A., *The Prophets*, vols. I and II (New York, Harper and Row, 1962).

Hillers, D. R., *Micah* (Fortress, Philadelphia, 1984).

Hobbs, T. R., *2 Kings* (Waco, Word, 1985).

Hobbs, T. R., 'Some Remarks on the Composition and Structure of the Book of Jeremiah', *CBQ*, 34, 1972, pp. 257–275.

Hoffmann, H.-D., *Reform und Reformen: Untersuchungen zu einem Grundthema in der deuteronomistischen Geschichtsschreibung* (Zürich, Theologischer Verlag, 1980).

Holladay, W. L., *The Architecture of Jeremiah 1–20* (Associated University Presses, 1976).

Holladay, W. L., 'A Coherent Chronology of Jeremiah's Early Career', in P. M. Bogaert (ed.), *Le Livre de Jérémie* (Leuven University Press, 1981), pp. 58–79.

Holladay, W. L., *Jeremiah*, vol. I (Philadelphia, Fortress, 1986).

Holladay, W. L., *Jeremiah*, vol. II (Minneapolis, Augsburg Fortress, 1989).

Holt, E. K., 'The Chicken and the Egg – or: Was Jeremiah a Member of the Deuteronomist Party?' *JSOT*, 44, 1989, pp. 109–122.

Hubmann, F. D., *Untersuchungen zu den Konfessionen Jer 11:8 – 12:6 und 15:10–21* (Würzburg, Echter Verlag, 1978).

Hyatt, J. P., 'The Book of Jeremiah', *IB*, vol. 5 (New York, Abingdon, 1956), pp. 775–1142.

Hyatt, J. P., 'The Deuteronomic Edition of Jeremiah', *VSH*, 1, 1951, pp. 71–95.

Ittmann, N., *Die Konfessionen Jeremias*, WMANT 54 (Neukirchener Verlag, 1981).

Janssen, E., *Juda in der Exilszeit*, FRLANT 51 (Göttingen, Vandenhoeck und Ruprecht, 1956).

Janzen, J. G., *Studies in the Text of Jeremiah* (Cambridge, Mass., Harvard University Press, 1973).

Jobling, D., 'The Quest of the Historical Jeremiah', in P. M. Bogaert (ed.), *Le Livre de Jérémie*, pp. 285–297.

Keil, C. F., *Jeremiah and Lamentations* (Grand Rapids, Eerdmans, 1973).

Kessler, M., 'Jeremiah Chapters 26 – 45 Reconsidered', *JNES*, 27, 1968, pp. 81–88.

Kessler, M., 'The Significance of Jeremiah 36', *ZAW*, 81, 1969, pp. 381–383.

Klein, R. W., *Israel in Exile* (Philadelphia, Fortress, 1979).

Koch, K., *The Prophets*, vol. 2 (SCM, 1983).

Kraus, H.-J., *Worship in Israel: a Cultic History of the Old Testament* (Oxford, Basil Blackwell, 1966).

Kugel, J. L., *The Idea of Biblical Poetry* (New Haven, Yale University Press, 1981).

Lacocque, A., *The Book of Daniel* (SPCK, 1979).

Lemche, N. P., *Ancient Israel: a New History of Israelite Society* (Sheffield, JSOT Press, 1988).

Lewin, E. D., 'Arguing for Authority: Rhetorical Study of Jeremiah 1:4–18 and 20:7–18', *JSOT*, 32, 1985, pp. 105–119.

Lohfink, N., 'Der junge Jeremia als Propagandist und Poet: Zum Grundstock von Jer. 30–31', in P. M. Bogaert, *Le Livre de Jérémie*, pp. 351–368.

Long, B. O., 'Prophetic Authority as Social Reality', in G. W. Coats and Long, *Canon and Authority* (Philadelphia, Fortress, 1977), pp. 3–20.

Lundbom, J. R., *Jeremiah: a Study in Ancient Hebrew Rhetoric*, SBL Diss. 18 (Missoula, Scholars Press, 1975).

Lust, J., '"Gathering and return" in Jeremiah and Ezekiel', in P. M. Bogaert (ed.), *Le Livre de Jérémie*, pp. 119–142.

McConville, J. G., 'Ezra-Nehemiah and the Fulfilment of Prophecy', *VT*, 36, 1986, pp. 205–224.

McConville, J. G., 'Jeremiah: Prophet and Book', *TB*, 42, 1991, pp. 80–95.

McConville, J. G., 'I Kings viii 46–53 and the Deuteronomic Hope', *VT*, 42, 1992, pp. 67–79.

McConville, J. G., *Law and Theology in Deuteronomy* (Sheffield, JSOT Press, 1984).

McConville, J. G., 'Narrative and Meaning in the Books of Kings', *Biblica*, 70, 1989, pp. 31–49.

McKane, W., *Jeremiah*, ICC, vol. 1 (Edinburgh, T. and T. Clark, 1986).

McKane, W., 'Poetry and Prose in the Book of Jeremiah, with Special Reference to Jeremiah 3:6–11 and 12:14–17', *SVT*, 23, 1980, pp. 220–237.

Mauser, U., *Gottesbild und Menschwerdung* (Tübingen, Mohr, 1971).

Mays, J. L., *Hosea*, OTL (SCM, 1969).

Mendenhall, G. E., 'Covenant Forms in Israelite Tradition', *BA*, 17, 1954, pp. 50–76.

Mendenhall, G. E., *Law and Covenant in the Ancient Near East* (Pittsburgh, Biblical Colloquium, 1955).

Milgrom, J., 'The Date of Jeremiah, Chapter 2', *JNES*, 14, 1955, pp. 65–69.

Miller, J. W., *Das Verhältnis Jeremias und Hesekiels Sprachlich und Theologisch Untersucht* (Assen, van Gorcum, 1955).

Moberly, R. W. L., *At the Mountain of God* (Sheffield, JSOT Press, 1983).

Mowinckel, S., *Prophecy and Tradition: the Prophetic Books in the Light of the Study of the Growth and History of the Tradition* (Kristiania, Jacob Dybwad, 1946).

Mowinckel, S., *Zur Komposition des Buches Jeremia* (Kristiania, Jacob Dybwad, 1914).

Muilenburg, J., 'The "Office" of the Prophet in Ancient Israel', in J. P. Hyatt (ed.), *The Bible in Modern Scholarship* (Abingdon, 1965), pp. 74–97.

Nelson R. D., *The Double Redaction of the Deuteronomistic History* (Sheffield, JSOT Press, 1981).

Nicholson, E. W., *Deuteronomy and Tradition* (Oxford, Basil Blackwell, 1967).

Nicholson, E. W., *Preaching to the Exiles: a Study of the Prose Tradition in the Book of Jeremiah* (Oxford, Basil Blackwell, 1970).

Noth, M., *The Deuteronomistic History* (Sheffield, JSOT Press, 1981).

Noth, M., 'Office and Vocation in the Old Testament', in *The Laws in the Pentateuch and other Studies* (SCM, 1984), pp. 229–249.

O'Connor, K. M., '"Do not Trim a Word": The Contributions of Chapter 26 to the Book of Jeremiah', *CBQ*, 51, 1989, pp. 617–630.

O'Connor, K. M., *The Confessions of Jeremiah: their Interpretation and Role in Chapters 1–25*, SBL Dissertations 94 (Atlanta, Scholars Press, 1988).

Overholt, T. W., 'The End of Prophecy: No Players without a Program', *JSOT*, 42, 1988, pp. 103–115.

Overholt, T. W., 'The Falsehood of Idolatry: an Interpretation of Jeremiah x. 1–16', *JTS*, 16, 1965, pp. 1–12.

Overholt, T. W., *The Threat of Falsehood* (SCM, 1970).

Perdue, L. G. and Kovacs, B. W. (eds.), *A Prophet to the Nations: Essays in Jeremiah Studies* (Winona Lake, Eisenbrauns, 1984).

Petersen, D. L., *The Roles of Israel's Prophets* (Sheffield, JSOT Press, 1981).

Pohlmann, K.-F., 'Erwägungen zum Schlusskapitel des deuteronomistischen Geschichtswerkes', in FSE. Würthwein, A. H. J. Gunneweg and O. Kaiser (eds.), *Textgemäss* (Göttingen, Vandenhoeck und Ruprecht, 1979), pp. 94–109.

Pohlmann, K.-F., *Studien zum Jeremiabuch: ein Beitrag zur Frage nach der Entstehung des Jeremiabuches*, FRLANT 118 (Göttingen, Vandenhoeck und Ruprecht, 1978).

Polk, T., *The Prophetic Persona* (Sheffield, JSOT Press, 1984).

Polzin, R., *Moses and the Deuteronomist* (New York, Seabury, 1980).

Rad, von. G., *Deuteronomy*, OTL (SCM, 1966).

Rad, von. G., *Genesis*, OTL (1961).

Rad, von. G., *Old Testament Theology*, vols. I and II (Edinburgh and London, Oliver and Boyd, 1962, 1965).

Rad, von. G., *Studies in Deuteronomy* (SCM, 1953).

Raitt, T. M., *A Theology of Exile: Judgment/Deliverance in Jeremiah and Ezekiel* (Philadelphia, Fortress, 1977).

Rendtorff, R., *The Problem of the Process of Transmission of the Pentateuch* (Sheffield, JSOT Press, 1990).

Reventlow, H. G., *Das Amt des Propheten bei Amos*, FRLANT 80 (Göttingen, Vandenhoeck und Ruprecht, 1980).

Reventlow, H. G., *Liturgie und Prophetisches Ich bei Jeremia* (Gütersloh, Mohn, 1963).

Rietzschel, C., *Das problem der Urrolle* (Gütersloh, Mohn, 1966).

Robinson, H. W., *The Religious Ideas of the Old Testament* (Duckworth, 1913).

Robinson, J. A. T., *The Priority of John* (SCM, 1985).

Robinson, Th. 'Baruch's Roll', *ZAW*, 42, 1924, pp. 209–221.

Rudolph, W., *Jeremia*, HAT (Tübingen, Mohr, 1947).

Schenker, A., 'Unwiderrufliche Umkehr und neuer Bund. Vergleich zwischen der Wiederherstellung Israels in Dt. 4, 25–31; 30, 1–14 und dem neuen Bund in Jer 31, 31–34', *FZPT*, 27, 1980, pp. 93–106.

Seitz, C. R., 'The Prophet Moses and the Canonical Shape of Jeremiah', *ZAW*, 101, 1989, pp. 3–27.

Seitz, C. R., *Theology in Conflict: Reactions of the Exile in the Book of Jeremiah* (Berlin and New York, de Gruyter, 1988).

Skinner, J. S., *Prophecy and Religion* (Cambridge, Cambridge University Press, 1922).

201

Smith, M. S., *The Laments of Jeremiah and their Contexts*, SBL Monographs (Atlanta, Scholars Press, 1990).

Stulman, L., *The Prose Sermons of the Book of Jeremiah*, SBL Diss, 83 (Atlanta, Georgia, Scholars Press, 1986).

Sturdy, J. V. M., 'The Authorship of the "Prose Sermons" of Jeremiah', in *Prophecy*, Essays presented to G. Fohrer (Berlin, de Gruyter, 1980), pp. 143–150.

Thiel, W., *Die deuteronomistische Redaktion von Jeremia 1–25*, WMANT 41 (Neukirchen, Neukirchener Verlag, 1973).

Thiel, W., *Die deuteronomistische Redaktion von Jeremia 26–45*, WMANT 52 (Neukirchen, Neukirchener Verlag, 1981).

Thompson, J. A., *The Book of Jeremiah*, NICOT (Grand Rapids, Eerdmans, 1980).

Tov, E., 'Some Aspects of the Textual and Literary History of the Book of Jeremiah', in P. M. Bogaert, *Le Livre de Jérémie*, pp. 145–167.

Unterman, J., *From Repentance to Redemption: Jeremiah's Thought in Transition* (Sheffield, JSOT Press, 1987).

Volz, P., *Der Prophet Jeremia*, *KAT* (Leipzig, Deichert, 1928).

Wambacq, 'Jérémie, X, 1–16', *RB*, 81, 1974, pp. 57–62.

Wanke, G., *Untersuchungen zur sogenannten Baruchschrift*, *BZAW*, 122 (Berlin, de Gruyter, 1971).

Webb, B., *The Book of the Judges* (Sheffield, JSOT Press, 1987).

Weinfeld, M., *Deuteronomy and the Deuteronomic School* (Oxford, Clarendon Press, 1972).

Weippert, H., 'Der Beitrag Ausserbiblischer Prophetentexte zum Verständnis der Prosareden des Jeremiabuches', in P. M. Bogaert, *Le Livre de Jérémie*, pp. 83–104.

Weippert, H., *Die Prosareden des Jeremiabuches*, *BZAW*, 132 (Berlin de Gruyter, 1973).

Weiser, A., *Das Buch des Propheten Jeremia*, ATD (Göttingen, Vandenhoeck und Ruprecht, 1969).

Weiser, A., *Introduction to the Old Testament* (Darton, Longman and Todd, 1961).

Wenham, G. J., *Genesis 1–15* (Waco, Word, 1987).

Westermann, C., *Basic Forms of Prophetic Speech* (Lutterworth, 1967).

Westermann, C., *Genesis 12–36* (SPCK, 1986).

Westermann, C., *Praise and Lament in the Psalms* (Edinburgh, T. and T. Clark, 1961).

Wilson, R. R., 'An Interpretation of Ezekiel's Dumbness', *VT*, 22, 1972, pp. 91–104.

Wilson, R. R., *Prophecy and Society in Ancient Israel* (Philadelphia, Fortress, 1980).

Wolff, H. W., *Hosea: a Commentary on the Book of the Prophet Hosea* (Philadelphia, Fortress, 1974).

Wolff, H. W., *Joel and Amos* (Philadelphia, Fortress, 1987).

Index of authors

Index of subjects